STUDENT UNIT G

AS Chemistry
UNIT 1

Edexcel
Nuffield

Unit 1: Introductory Chemistry

Frank Harriss and Philip Jackson

Philip Allan Updates
Market Place
Deddington
Oxfordshire
OX15 0SE

tel: 01869 338652
fax: 01869 337590
e-mail: sales@philipallan.co.uk
www.philipallan.co.uk

ISBN-13: 978-0-86003-935-8
ISBN-10: 0-86003-935-8

This guide has been written specifically to support students preparing for the Edexcel Nuffield AS Chemistry Unit 1 examination. The content has been neither approved nor endorsed by Edexcel and remains the sole responsibility of the authors.

Printed by MPG Books, Bodmin

P00615

Contents

Introduction

About this guide

This guide is designed to help you prepare for the first Nuffield AS Chemistry unit test, which examines the content of **Unit 1: Introductory Chemistry**.

The aim of this guide is to provide you with a clear understanding of the requirements of the unit and to advise you on how best to meet those requirements.

The book is divided into the following sections:

- This **Introduction**, which outlines revision and examination technique, showing you how to prepare for the unit test.
- **Content Guidance**, which provides a summary of all the 'chemical ideas' covered in Unit 1.
- **Questions and Answers**, in which you will find questions in the same style as in the unit test, followed by the answers of two students, one of whom is likely to get an A grade, the other a C/D grade. Examiner's comments follow each of these answers.

How to use this guide

- Begin by reading the section 'Revision and examination technique' in this Introduction.
- Decide on the amount of time you have available for chemistry revision.
- Allocate suitable amounts of time to:
  - each section of the Content Guidance, giving the most time to the areas that seem most unfamiliar
  - the questions in the Questions and Answers section
- Draw up a revision timetable, allocating the time for questions later in your timetable.
- When revising sections of the Content Guidance:
  - read the guidance and look at corresponding sections in your notes and textbooks
  - write your own revision notes
  - try questions from past unit tests and from other sources, such as the *Students' Book*
- When using the Questions and Answers:
  - try to answer the question yourself
  - then look at the students' answers, together with your own, and try to work out the best answer
  - then look at the examiner's comments

Revision and examination technique

How do I find what to learn?

Well, we hope this book will be useful to you! Other sources are:

- the specification. This is the definitive one. If it's not in the specification, it won't be in the paper! However, the specification is written in 'examiner-speak', so it might not always be absolutely clear what is required. This guide should help you to interpret the unit content — every specification point is covered in the Content Guidance section.
- the summaries of Key Principles at the end of the topics in the *Students' Book*.
- your own and your teacher's notes. Preparation for an exam is not just something you do shortly before you take the paper. It should be an integral part of your daily work in chemistry.

How much of the *Students' Book* do I need to learn?

You will need most of this, except:

- the fine detail of experimental procedure
- background reading

General revision tips

Revision is a very personal thing

What works for one person does not necessarily work for another. You should by now have some idea about what methods suit you, but here are a few ways to set out your revision notes:

- mind maps — ideas radiate out from a central point and are linked together; some people like to colour these in
- notes with bullet points and headings
- small cards with a limited 'bite-size' amount of material on each

Make a plan

Divide up your material into sections (the Content Guidance section will be very helpful here). Then:

- work out how much time you have available before the exam
- allocate each section as much time as you can, bearing in mind which you feel you nearly understand and which are the most difficult
- fit this in with any revision your teacher is going to do — ask him or her for a summary

Write, write, write!

Whatever you do, make sure that your revision is *active*, not just flipping over the pages saying 'yeah, yeah, I know this already'. Write more revision notes, test yourself (or each other), *try questions*.

Test yourself

- The review questions in the *Students' Book* are useful 'drill exercises' on topics, but are not all like exam questions.
- Past papers are available and they give you a very good indication of what you will be facing.
- The Questions and Answers section of this book is designed for this purpose.

Know the enemy — the exam paper

Hopefully, since you will have prepared properly, you will be able to look on the exam as an opportunity to show what you can do, rather than as a battle! Be aware, however, that you must prepare yourself for an exam just as you would for an important sporting contest — be focused. Work hard right through the 75 minutes and don't dwell on difficulties — put them behind you. Try to emerge feeling worn out but happy that you have done your very best, even if you have found it difficult (others will probably feel the same way). Then forget it and don't have a post-mortem.

Sections A and B

Section A consists of *about* four unrelated short-answer questions. There are *about* 12 marks for these questions. Section B contains *about* five questions, worth the remainder of the 60 marks. Each of these questions has a 'theme' and includes both short-answer and longer-answer parts.

Nuffield is all about learning chemistry through experiment, so it is right that the exam questions should reflect this. However, some will be based on chemistry in everyday life and others will be more theoretical.

Sometimes the context will come from the *Students' Book*, sometimes it will be a new one. Look carefully at the 'stem' (the introduction at the top of the question). Most of the important facts here will be needed somewhere in the question. Sometimes, small, additional stems are added later on. These are important too.

60 marks in 75 minutes

It is important to pace yourself through the paper so you can tell whether you are ahead of, or behind, the clock. It is best to work through the paper in order, from the beginning to the end, since section A often contains relatively straightforward questions.

50/10 knowledge/application of knowledge

This one you may not know about. Of the total, 50 marks test your knowledge and ask about things you will have learned. The other 10 marks are for the application of that knowledge to new situations or through doing calculations. These questions often begin with 'Suggest...' to make it clear that you are not expected to be able to recall the answer. There are approximately the same number of marks allocated to each of the five topics covered in the *Students' Book*.

Easy and hard parts

The papers are designed so that, ideally, an A-grade candidate will get 80% (48 out of 60) and an E-grade candidate 40% (24 out of 60). The actual mark for each grade varies between papers, depending on the difficulty, and is only decided after all the papers have been marked. Some of the parts are designed with A-grade candidates in mind and so will seem quite demanding. Other parts are designed to allow an E-grade candidate to score 40% and so will seem rather easy. Thus, there are easy, middling and hard parts within each question.

Dealing with different types of question

Short-answer questions

These are the most straightforward, but remember:

- look at the marks available — make one good point per mark.
- look at the number of lines — this gives *some* idea of the length of answer required. Of course, handwriting varies greatly in size, but if you have written two words and there are three lines, you can assume you have not written enough to score full marks!
- don't 'hedge your bets' — if you give two alternative answers, you will not get the marks unless *both* are right. For example, if the answer is 'hydrogen bond' and you write 'hydrogen bond or permanent dipole–permanent dipole force', you will score zero.
- read the question — don't answer a question that you have made up! Examiners do have kind hearts really, and they are genuinely sorry when they have to award zero for an answer containing good chemistry that is not relevant to the question asked. This is a problem with units that are examined twice a year. There are lots of past papers around, all asking slightly different questions on the same subject-matter. It's all too easy to give the answer to last year's question.

Longer-answer questions

The same rules apply about marks, lines and reading the question. In addition:

- think before you write — perhaps jot down a few points in the margin. Try to make your points logically.
- punch those points — if you have read any mark-schemes you will see that they give examiners advice on the weakest answer that will still just score the mark. Make sure your points are made well and win the mark without requiring a second's hesitation by the examiner.
- try to write clear sentences (though bullet points might be appropriate on some occasions).
- be sure you do not re-state the question, i.e. don't use words or phrases directly from the question as part of your explanation.

Command words in questions

A lot of care is taken in choosing which of these words to use, so note them carefully:

- 'state', 'write down', 'give' and 'name' require short answers only
- 'describe' requires an accurate account of the main points, but no explanation
- 'explain' requires chemical reasons for the statement given
- 'suggest' means that you are not expected to know the answer but you should be able to work it out from what you do know

- 'giving reason(s)' requires you to explain why you chose to answer as you did (if 'reasons' in the plural is stated, judge the number required from the number of marks)

Avoid vague answers

Sometimes it is clear that the candidate knows quite a lot about the topic but his or her answer is not focused. Avoid these words:

- 'it' (e.g. 'it is bigger') — give the name of the thing you are describing, otherwise it may not be very clear which object in the question is being referred to
- 'harmful' — if you mean 'toxic' or 'poisonous', say so!
- 'environmentally friendly' — say *why* it benefits the environment
- 'expensive' — always justify this word with a reason

Be careful with chemical particles — always think twice whenever you write 'particle', 'atom', 'molecule' or 'ion', and check that you are using the correct term.

If in doubt, write something

Try to avoid leaving any gaps. Have a go at every answer. If you are not sure, write something that seems to be sensible chemistry. As you will see from the Questions and Answers section, some questions have a variety of possible answers — the only answer that definitely scores zero is a blank.

Diagrams

You would be amazed at some of the diagrams examiners have to mark, so please:

- read the question. The answer is not always a reflux condenser! If it is an apparatus you know, then it is relatively straightforward. If you have to design something, look for clues in the question.
- make it clear and neat. Use a pencil and a ruler, and have a soft rubber handy to erase any errors.
- make sure it looks like real apparatus (which never has square corners, for example). Some apparatus drawn in exams would test the skill of the most proficient glass-blower.
- draw a cross-section, so that gases can have a clear path through. Don't carelessly leave any gaps where gases could leak out.
- think of safety. Don't suggest heating an enclosed apparatus, which would explode. If a poisonous gas is given off, show it being released in a fume cupboard.
- always label your diagram, especially if the question tells you to. Important things to label are substances and calibrated vessels (e.g. syringes or measuring cylinders).

Calculations

It is always very easy to make mistakes, especially under the pressure of exams. So, set out the steps in your calculations clearly. Then you will get most of the marks if you make a slight mistake and the examiner can see what you are doing. Examiners operate a system called 'transferred error' whereby, once an error has been made, the rest of the calculation scores marks if the method is correct from then on.

When you write down your numerical answer, check:

- **units** — most physical quantities have them, for example $g\,mol^{-1}$, $kJ\,mol^{-1}$
- **sign** (remember that oxidation states and ΔH values must be shown as '+' if they are positive)
- **significant figures** — you may be expected to analyse uncertainties more carefully in your practical work, but in exam papers all you have to do is to give the same number of significant figures as the data in the question

Content Guidance

The material in this section summarises the chemical concepts from **Unit 1: Introductory Chemistry**. Note that each section of the Nuffield specification brings in chemical ideas from a variety of topic areas. This content guidance section is divided into chemical topics, which in some cases link ideas from more than one section of the specification.

Summary of content

About the atom: the make-up of an atom; isotopes; the mass spectrometer; flame colours and emission spectra; ionisation energies; electron arrangement

The periodic table: periodic trends of physical properties; similarities and trends in a group; group 2; making salts

Bonding and structure: ionic bonding; evidence for the existence of ions; atomic and ionic radius; metallic bonding; uses of metals

Organic chemistry: alkanes; alkenes; alcohols; aldehydes, ketones and carboxylic acids

Mole calculations and equations: moles of atoms and molecules; formulae; equations; types of reaction; calculations from equations; percentage yield

Enthalpy changes: measuring enthalpy changes; standard enthalpy changes; Hess's law

Acids and bases: definitions; strong and weak acids and bases; titrations; titration calculations

How much of this do I need to learn?

The answer is, virtually all of it. It has been pared down to the absolute essentials. If you need any more detail on any aspect, you should look in your textbooks or notes.

About the atom

The make-up of an atom

The nucleus of an atom consists of **protons** and **neutrons**. **Electrons** move around the nucleus. Their properties are shown in the table below:

Particle	Mass	Charge
Proton	1	+1
Neutron	1	0
Electron	Very small	–1

The number of these particles in an atom is indicated like this:

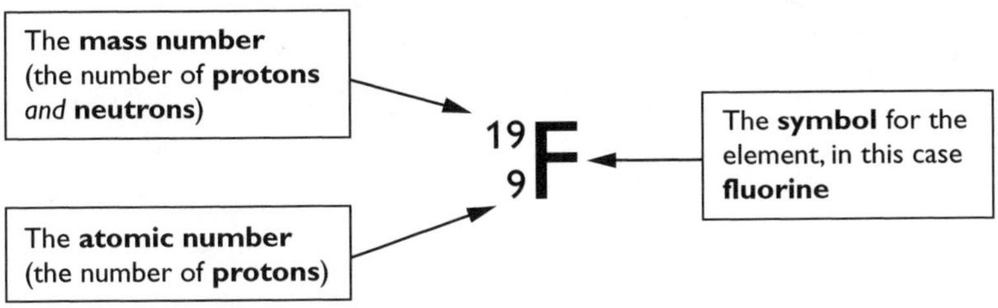

For a neutral atom, the number of electrons is equal to the number of protons.

Isotopes

Isotopes are different forms of the same element. Their atoms have the *same number of protons* but *different numbers of neutrons*. For example, hydrogen has *three isotopes*, $^{1}_{1}H$, $^{2}_{1}H$ and $^{3}_{1}H$. These all have one proton (otherwise they wouldn't be hydrogen) but they have zero, one and two neutrons respectively, as can be seen from the mass numbers.

The **relative atomic mass** of an atom is defined as the number of times one atom is heavier than one-twelfth of an atom of carbon-12 (the isotope $^{12}_{6}C$). For an element that consists of just one isotope (for example, fluorine), this means that the relative atomic mass is virtually the same as the **mass number** — in this case, 19.

However, when an element consists of two or more isotopes, the relative atomic mass is the mean (average) of the **relative isotopic masses**, taking into account the **relative abundances** (how much of each of them occurs naturally). For example, chlorine has two isotopes, $^{35}_{17}Cl$ (which makes up 75% of chlorine) and $^{37}_{17}Cl$ (which makes up the remaining 25%). The relative atomic mass is calculated like this:

$$\text{relative atomic mass} = \frac{(35 \times 75) + (37 \times 25)}{100} = 35.5$$

Practise these calculations! Relative abundance data for the isotopes of an element are in the *Nuffield Book of Data*.

Tip Read the question! If relative atomic mass is asked for, there are no units. Molar masses have units $g\,mol^{-1}$.

The mass spectrometer

The masses of atoms can be measured using a **mass spectrometer**. This works as shown in the following diagram.

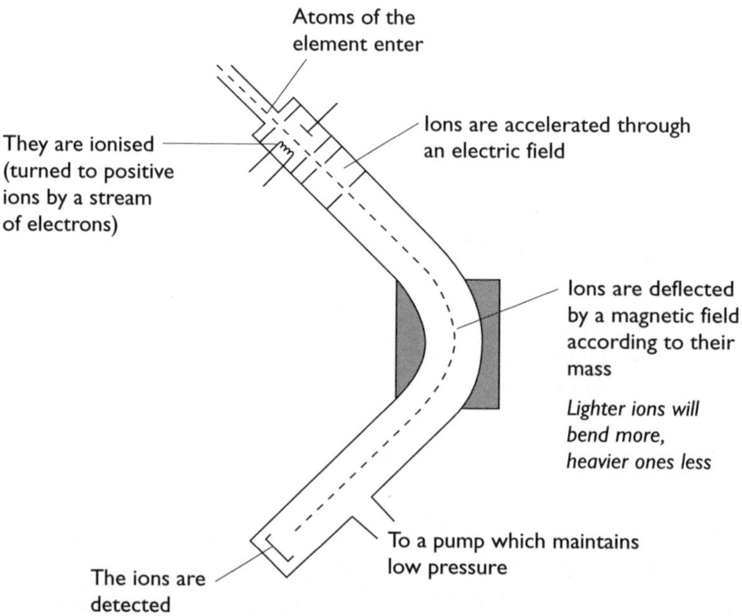

The magnetic field is varied so that ions of different mass hit the detector at different times. This enables a **mass spectrum** to be produced. The mass spectrum of bromine is shown below.

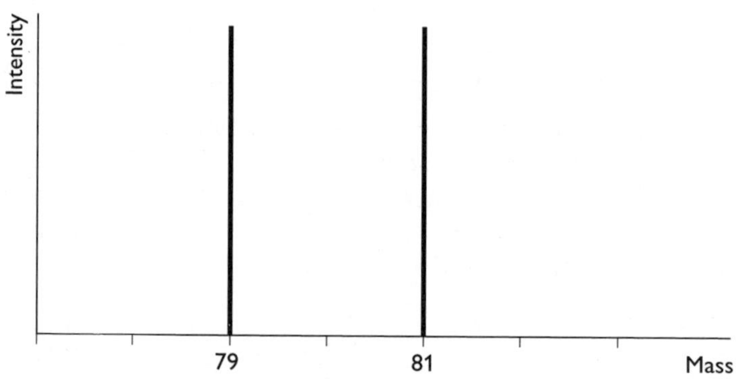

This shows that there are two isotopes, masses 79 and 81, of equal intensity. The molar mass is given by:

$$\frac{(79 \times 50) + (81 \times 50)}{100} = 80\,\text{g mol}^{-1}$$

Tip You are unlikely to be asked to draw a mass spectrometer, but you should know how it works and the type of information it can provide.

Flame colours and emission spectra

Flame colours

When an element gains energy, for instance from a Bunsen flame, it emits light of a particular colour. As the atoms gain energy, electrons are promoted from lower energy levels to higher energy levels. Then the electrons fall back to lower energy levels, emitting light of a specific wavelength. This gives rise to the characteristic flame colour for the element. This phenomenon is useful in analysing substances and has everyday applications, such as in sodium street lamps.

Element	Flame colour
Lithium	Red
Sodium	Yellow
Potassium	Lilac
Magnesium	Does not emit in the visible spectrum
Calcium	Red
Strontium	Crimson
Barium	Green

Tip You should learn the flame colours you have met.

Emission spectra

Electrons in an atom exist in definite energy levels. They cannot possess an intermediate amount of energy. The evidence for the existence of electron energy levels comes from a study of **line emission spectra**. The energy levels of a hydrogen atom are shown below — other atoms' energy levels are similar, though more complex.

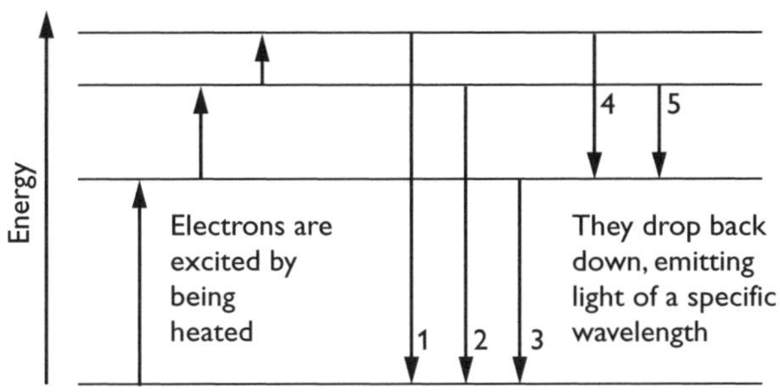

When electrons are excited by being heated, they move up energy levels; they then drop down to lower energy levels, giving out light of specific wavelengths. This gives rise to an **emission spectrum**, which consists of very fine coloured lines on a dark background.

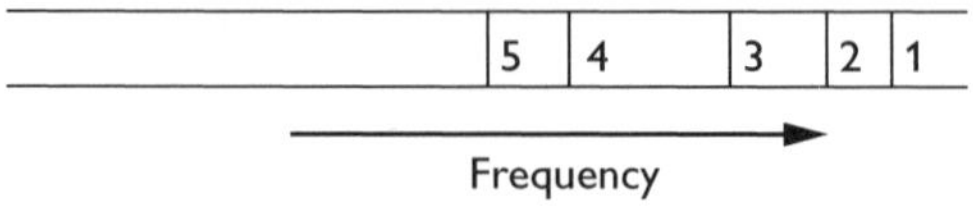

The line numbers correspond to the energy changes in the energy level diagram above.

Tip You may have to draw diagrams of energy levels and emission spectra like those above.

Ionisation energies

The **first ionisation energy** measures the amount of energy needed to remove 1 mole of electrons from *1 mole* of *gaseous* atoms to form *gaseous* ions:

$M(g) \longrightarrow M^{+}(g) + e^{-}$

The **second ionisation energy** measures the amount of energy needed to remove the second electron (*not* the first and the second electron) from *1 mole* of singly charged ions:

$M^{+}(g) \longrightarrow M^{2+}(g) + e^{-}$

Ionisation energy values depend on the **electronic structure**.

The ionisation energy is *lower* (i.e. the ion is formed with greater ease) when:

- the electron being removed is further from the nucleus (smaller pull) — thus *the first ionisation energy decreases down a group* as the outer electron shell gets further from the nucleus
- fewer protons are attracting electrons in the same shell (smaller pull again) — thus *the first ionisation energy increases across a period* as the number of protons in the nucleus increases

Electron arrangement

Examination of line emission spectra and ionisation energies gives information about the arrangement of electrons in energy levels. You know from GCSE that the first energy level (quantum shell) can contain a maximum of two electrons and that the second energy level can contain up to eight electrons. You may have been told that the third energy level also contains a maximum of eight electrons, but this is not actually true.

Sodium (atomic number 11) has its eleven electrons arranged 2, 8, 1. The electron in the third energy level is the most easily removed as relatively little energy is required to remove it from the atom. There is a big jump in ionisation energy to remove the next electron because a full energy level is being broken into. A graph of ionisation energy against the number of the electron it applies to does not reveal very much.

Much more useful is a graph of the logarithm of the ionisation energy (IE) against electron number, as shown below.

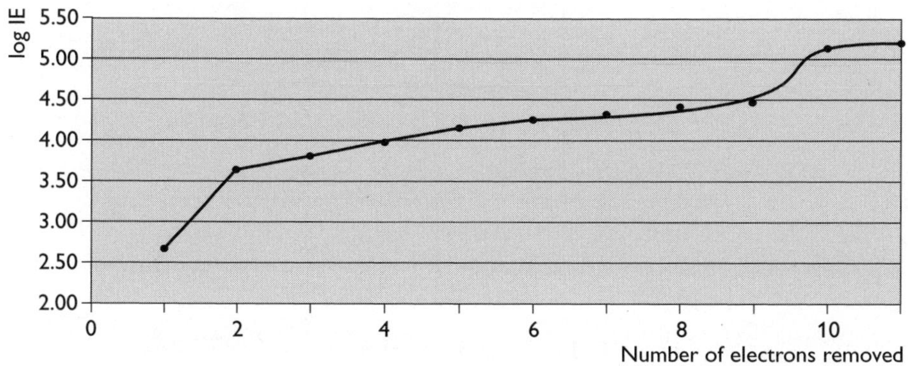

This graph shows:

- the big jump in ionisation energy from the first to the second electron as the second energy level is broken into
- a further jump between the ninth and tenth electrons as the first energy level is broken into

Tip Examiners are fond of asking you to sketch such graphs. Make sure you start at the right end!

This kind of information can be used to work out in which group an element occurs. In the following example, the first six ionisation energies (in kJ mol^{-1}) of an element are given.

Electron removed	Ionisation energy/kJ mol^{-1}
First	789
Second	1577
Third	3232
Fourth	4356
Fifth	16 091
Sixth	19 785

There is a big jump between the fourth and fifth ionisation energies. The first four electrons are relatively easy to remove. Therefore, the element is in group 4.

Closer examination of the emission spectra shows that the energy levels are split into sub-shells, called *s, p, d* and *f*. The energy level number tells us how many sub-shells it contains:

- The first energy level has one sub-shell, 1*s*, which can contain two electrons.
- The second energy level has two sub-shells — 2*s*, which can contain two electrons, and 2*p*, which can contain up to six.

Energy level	Sub-shell	Number of electrons
1	s	2
2	s *p*	2 6
3	s *p* *d*	2 6 10
4	s *p* *d* *f*	2 6 10 14

Thus the electron configuration of bromine (atomic number 35), which can be written as 2, 8, 18, 7, is more accurately represented by:

$1s^2\ 2s^2\ 2p^6\ 3s^2\ 3p^6\ 3d^{10}\ 4s^2\ 4p^5$

Elements in the same group of the periodic table have the same outer electron arrangement.

Group 2 element	Electron configuration
Beryllium	$1s^2\ 2s^2$
Magnesium	$1s^2\ 2s^2\ 2p^6\ 3s^2$
Calcium	$1s^2\ 2s^2\ 2p^6\ 3s^2\ 3p^6\ 4s^2$
Strontium	$1s^2\ 2s^2\ 2p^6\ 3s^2\ 3p^6\ 3d^{10}\ 4s^2\ 4p^6\ 5s^2$
Barium	$1s^2\ 2s^2\ 2p^6\ 3s^2\ 3p^6\ 3d^{10}\ 4s^2\ 4p^6\ 4d^{10}\ 5s^2\ 5p^6\ 6s^2$

It is because of these outer electrons that elements in a group have similar chemical properties.

The group number of an element is given by the total number of *s*- and *p*-electrons in its outer shell. Thus, nitrogen (atomic number 7) is $1s^2\ 2s^2\ 2p^3$ and is therefore in group 5 (2 + 3).

Electron affinity

Atoms can also gain electrons. The **electron affinity** is the energy change when each atom in *1 mole* of gaseous atoms gains an electron to become a *singly charged* gaseous anion.

$Cl(g) + e^- \longrightarrow Cl^-(g) \quad E_{aff} = -349\,kJ\,mol^{-1}$

The periodic table

The periodic table lists the elements in order of **atomic number** and groups elements together according to their common properties.

Periodic trends of physical properties

Melting points and **boiling points** of the elements are said to show **periodic trends** since the pattern of rise and fall is repeated as you go across the elements of each period. This is because the bonding of the elements changes from **metallic** to **giant covalent** to **covalent molecules** as we go from left to right across a period (see the section on 'Bonding'). The **electrical conductivity** is high where there are metals on the left of a period but drops markedly on the right of a period where the elements are non-metals.

First ionisation energies also show a periodic trend, as shown in the graph below.

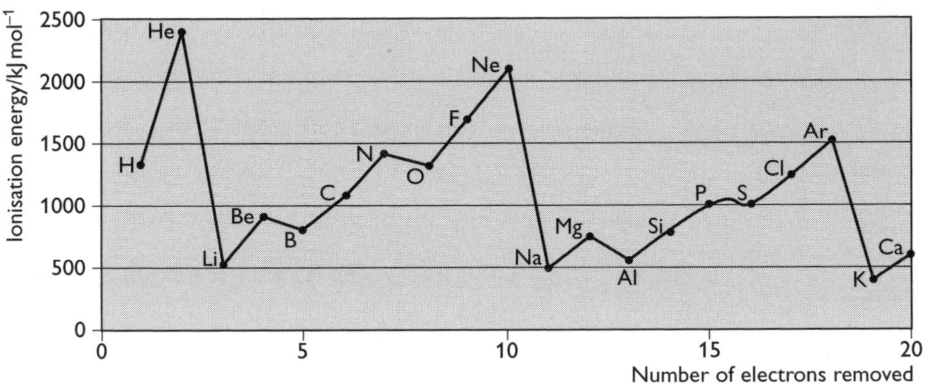

The noble gases occur at the peaks of the graph and the group 1 metals in the troughs. There is a general increase across a period, which is repeated in the next. Where there are dips in one period they too are repeated in the next.

Tip Examiners often ask you to draw such a graph for a period. For full marks you need to know where the dips occur (e.g. for boron and oxygen in the second short period).

Similarities and trends in a group

Because elements in the same group have the same number of outer-shell electrons, they tend to react in the same way. Thus they form ions with the same charge and molecules with the same general formulae (see the section on 'Bonding'). As we go down the group, the electrons are further from the nucleus and are more easily lost. Thus the elements become *more* metallic (for example, the alkali metals) or *less non-metallic* (for example, the halogens).

Group 2

As we go down the group from magnesium to calcium, strontium and barium, the elements become more metallic as their ionisation energies become smaller.

Reactions with water

The elements get *more reactive* down the group:

$M(s) + 2H_2O(l) \longrightarrow M(OH)_2(aq) + H_2(g)$

Oxides and hydroxides

The oxides all react with water to form *alkaline* hydroxides.

$MO(s) + H_2O(l) \longrightarrow M(OH)_2(aq)$

The oxides and hydroxides are also *bases* since they react with acids to neutralise them. For example:

$MO(s) + 2HCl(aq) \longrightarrow MCl_2(aq) + H_2O(l)$

and

$M(OH)_2(s) + 2HCl(aq) \longrightarrow MCl_2(aq) + 2H_2O(l)$

The hydroxides become *more soluble* down the group.

Carbonates

All the group 2 carbonates decompose on heating:

$MCO_3(s) \longrightarrow MO(s) + CO_2(g)$

Barium carbonate needs the highest temperature, so it is said to have the highest **thermal stability**.

All the carbonates are insoluble in water but they become *less soluble* down the group. Notice that this is the opposite way round from the hydroxides.

Nitrates

All the group 2 nitrates decompose on heating, losing their water of crystallisation first. For example:

$2Mg(NO_3)_2(s) \longrightarrow 2MgO(s) + 4NO_2(g) + O_2(g)$

The trend in thermal stability is the same as for the carbonates — increasing as the group is descended.

Making salts

Making a soluble salt involves adding a metal, a base or a carbonate to an acid.

- acid + metal ⟶ salt + hydrogen
  e.g. $2HCl(aq) + Mg(s) \longrightarrow MgCl_2(aq) + H_2(g)$
- acid + base ⟶ salt + water
  e.g. $H_2SO_4(aq) + 2NaOH(aq) \longrightarrow Na_2SO_4(aq) + 2H_2O(l)$
- acid + carbonate ⟶ salt + water + carbon dioxide
  e.g. $2HNO_3(aq) + CaCO_3(s) \longrightarrow Ca(NO_3)_2(aq) + 2H_2O(l) + CO_2(g)$

Tip You could be asked to write balanced equations like these, in which you will be expected to get the state symbols right.

Practical points

Examiners often ask you to describe the preparation of pure, dry, hydrated crystals.

- Usually excess solid is added to the acid to make sure that all the acid is used up.
- The excess solid is then filtered off.
- The filtrate (which is the solution of the salt) is then concentrated to crystallisation point by heating in an evaporating dish. All the water is *not* boiled off in one go, especially if it is the hydrated salt that is required. If all the water is boiled off, the water of crystallisation is lost, leaving just a powder.
- The remaining filtrate is left to crystallise slowly.
- Pure dry crystals are obtained by filtering to remove any remaining solution and then drying between pieces of filter paper — not in an oven, because this would remove the water of crystallisation.

Bonding and structure

Ionic bonding

When a metal and a non-metal combine, they usually form an **ionic** compound. Elements combine in order to lose energy. Often the ions formed have the full electron arrangement of the nearest noble gas. Metals (being on the left of the periodic table) can most easily do this by *losing electrons* to form positive **cations**. Non-metals *gain electrons* to form negative **anions**. The charges on ions formed by a single element can be related to their position in the periodic table. Carbonate, nitrate and sulphate contain more than one non-metal and their formulae have to be learnt — but no chemist should be ignorant of these.

H **H^+ and H^-**							He
Li **Li^+**	Be	B	C	N **N^{3-}**	O **O^{2-}**	F **F^-**	Ne
Na **Na^+**	Mg **Mg^{2+}**	Al **Al^{3+}**	Si	P **P^{3-}**	S **S^{2-}**	Cl **Cl^-**	Ar
K **K^+**	Ca **Ca^{2+}**		**CO_3^{2-}** carbonate	**NO_3^-** nitrate **NH_4^+** ammonium	**SO_4^{2-}** sulphate		

Tip The charges on common ions should be learnt.

When forming ionic compounds, electrons are transferred so that both atoms gain a full outer shell. This can be shown by **dot-and-cross diagrams**, which show only the outer-shell electrons.

For example, magnesium has two outer-shell electrons. It can give one (shown as × in the diagram below) to each of *two* chlorine atoms to make magnesium chloride, $MgCl_2$.

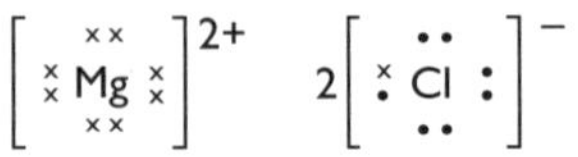

Evidence for the existence of ions

Losing electrons creates positive ions (cations). Gaining electrons produces negative ions (anions).

The evidence for the existence of ions in compounds is as follows:

- Salt solutions conduct electricity — the movement of charged particles through solutions or molten liquids is evidence for the presence of ions.
- Charged particles can be shown to migrate as a result of an electrical potential being applied to a coloured salt solution.

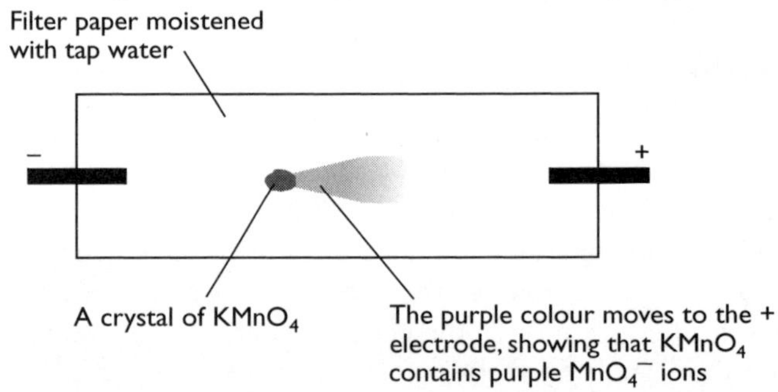

Atomic and ionic radius

The size of an atom is determined by the electrostatic attraction of the positively charged nucleus for the negatively charged electrons and the electrostatic repulsion the electrons exert on each other. The nucleus pulls the electrons in until the attraction is balanced by the repulsive forces between the electrons.

Metal atoms lose electrons to form cations. Therefore, a cation has fewer electrons than the original atom, so the remaining electrons can be drawn in closer by the nucleus. Cations are therefore smaller than the atom from which they were made.

Non-metals gain electrons to form anions. Therefore, an anion has more electrons than the original atom and so the inter-electronic repulsions are increased. This means that the electrons can escape further from the nuclear pull. Anions are therefore bigger than the atom from which they were made.

Atomic and ionic radii increase down groups of the periodic table, as the number of full electron shells increases. Data for groups 1 and 7 are shown in the following tables.

Group 1

Element	Atomic radius/nm	Ionic radius/nm
Li	0.157	0.074
Na	0.191	0.102
K	0.235	0.138
Rb	0.250	0.149
Cs	0.272	0.170

Group 7

Element	Atomic radius/nm	Ionic radius/nm
F	0.071	0.133
Cl	0.099	0.180
Br	0.114	0.195
I	0.133	0.215

Across a period, the atomic radius decreases, as the increasing number of protons exerts an increased attraction on the electrons, which is not balanced by the increased number of electrons.

Be careful when comparing the sizes of ions, for example the N^{3-} ion and the O^{2-} ion. Both of these have the same number of electrons ($1s^2$, $2s^2$, $2p^6$) but the O^{2-} ion has one more proton and is therefore smaller.

The ionic radius of a cation affects the thermal stability of its salts. Nitrates and carbonates of the smaller group 2 cations, such as Mg^{2+}, are less stable (more easily decomposed) because they distort the anion. The thermal stability of group 2 nitrates and carbonates increases down the group as the cation radius increases.

Metallic bonding

In a metal structure, the outer-shell electrons of the metal atoms become detached from the atoms. Thus, metals consist of a **lattice** of positive ions. This accounts for their ability to bend and stretch without breaking, since the ions can move over each other in layers. The electrons can move around between the ions and are said to be **delocalised**. This causes the metal to conduct electricity. Think of 'cation islands in a sea of electrons'. The positively charged ions attract the negative electrons and this attraction holds the structure together.

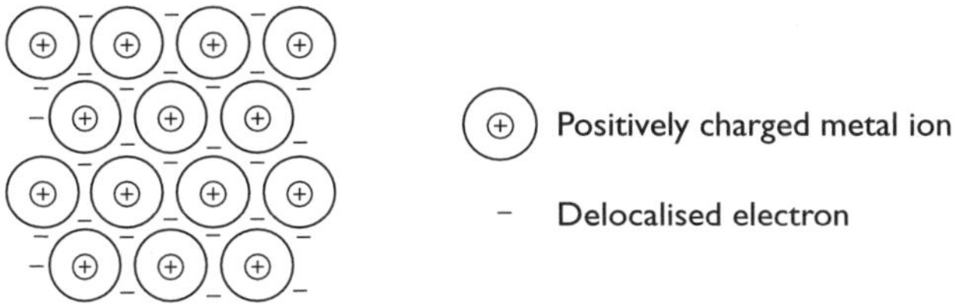

Tip Only one or two electrons are delocalised from each atom — make sure your diagram does not show too many electrons.

Uses of metals

- Metals are strong (because of their strong metallic bonding). For example, iron is used in steel for cars, bridges, building construction and so on.
- Metals are good conductors of electricity (because of the delocalised electrons in the metallic structure). For example, copper is used in electrical cables.

Organic chemistry

Alkanes

Alkanes are the series of hydrocarbons with the general formula C_nH_{2n+2}. This is an example of an **homologous series**.

The first member of the series is **methane**. Three ways of writing the formula of methane are shown below.

CH_4

Molecular formula

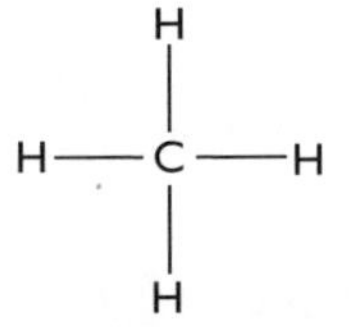

Displayed formula

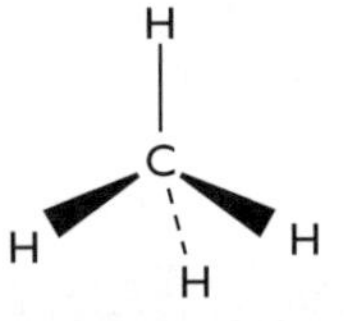

3-dimensional formula

The next five members of the series are given in the table below.

Alkane	Molecular formula
Ethane	C_2H_6
Propane	C_3H_8
Butane	C_4H_{10}
Pentane	C_5H_{12}
Hexane	C_6H_{14}

Tip You should learn these names.

- The **molecular formula** gives the number of each type of atom in a molecule of the substance.
- A **structural formula** shows the structure in a condensed form, for example CH_3CH_2OH.
- A **displayed formula** shows all the bonds and all the atoms.

The formulae of butane and pentane are shown in the following table.

Alkane	Molecular formula	Structural formula	Displayed formula
Butane	C_4H_{10}	$CH_3–CH_2–CH_2–CH_3$	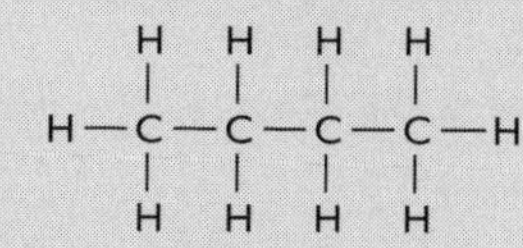
Pentane	C_5H_{12}	$CH_3–CH_2–CH_2–CH_2–CH_3$	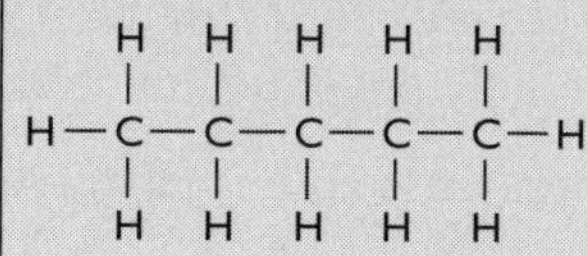

Tip When a question asks you to give the structure of a substance, make sure you give the type of formula asked for. Don't draw structures that are a mixture of structural and displayed formulae.

Alkenes

The alkenes are another homologous series of hydrocarbons. Alkenes have a carbon–carbon double bond and their general formula is C_nH_{2n}.

The formulae of ethene and propene are shown below.

Alkene	Molecular formula	Structural formula	Displayed formula
Ethene	C_2H_4	$CH_2=CH_2$	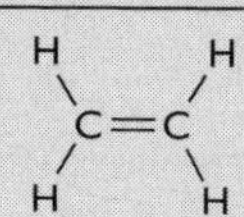
Propene	C_3H_6	$CH_2=CH–CH_3$	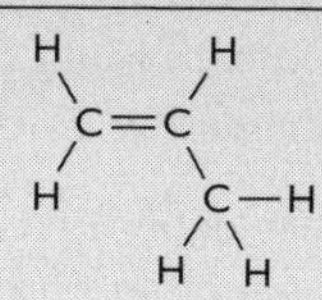

Alcohols

Alcohols, in which the **functional group –OH** replaces one of the hydrogen atoms of an alkane, are another homologous series.

The simplest alcohol is **methanol**, CH_3OH. The next in the series is **ethanol**, C_2H_5OH. After that, it gets a little more complicated, as there is more than one possible position for the –OH group. There are *two* possibilities for **propanol**. These can be shown using displayed formulae.

Propan-1-ol

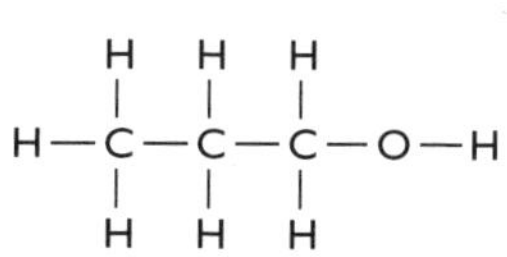

Propan-2-ol

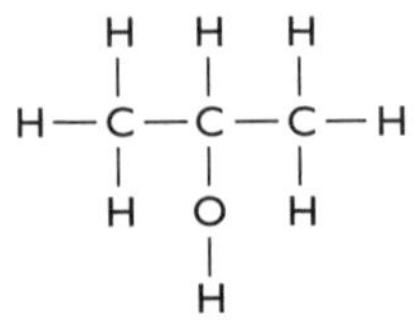

These are called **structural isomers** as they have the same molecular formula (C_3H_8O) but different structural formulae.

There are four isomers of **butanol**:

Structural formula	Name	Classification
$H_3C—CH_2—CH_2—CH_2—OH$	Butan-1-ol	Primary alcohol
$H_3C—CH_2—CH(OH)—CH_3$	Butan-2-ol	Secondary alcohol
$H_3C—C(CH_3)(OH)—CH_3$	2-methylpropan-2-ol	Tertiary alcohol
$H_3C—CH(CH_3)—CH_2—OH$	2-methylpentan-1-ol	Primary alcohol

Classifying alcohols

A **primary** alcohol has the –OH group attached to a carbon atom that is attached directly to *one* other carbon atom.

A **secondary** alcohol has the –OH group attached to a carbon atom that is attached directly to *two* other carbon atoms.

A **tertiary** alcohol has the –OH group attached to a carbon atom that is attached directly to *three* other carbon atoms.

Naming alcohols

To name an alcohol, follow these rules:

- Find the *longest* carbon chain. This may 'go round corners' depending on how the structure is drawn. The number of carbon atoms indicates the first part of the name — ethan-, propan-, butan- and so on.
- The –OH group is described by the number of the carbon atom to which it is attached — for example, propan-2-ol, 3-methylbutan-1-ol. Always number from the chain end nearest to the –OH group to keep the number as small as possible.
- If the chain is branched, indicate the branches like this: 2-methylpropan-1-ol.

Tip You only need to know enough of this naming procedure to enable you to name and recognise simple primary, secondary and tertiary alcohols.

Physical properties of alcohols

Alcohols are typical covalent molecules.

- The early members of the homologous series have low melting points (below room temperature) and relatively low boiling points (above room temperature).
- The first three members of the homologous series are soluble in water (miscible in all proportions). As the hydrocarbon chain becomes longer, the solubility decreases.
- They are neutral in aqueous solution because the –OH group does not form either H^+ or OH^- ions when the alcohol dissolves.

Chemical properties of alcohols

The chemistry of alcohols is essentially the chemistry of the functional group, –OH.

The strong C–H bonds attached to the carbon skeleton seldom break, so the reactions of alcohols involve the breaking of either the C–O or the O–H bond.

Alcohols are flammable and burn to produce carbon dioxide and water.

$$C_2H_5OH + 3O_2 \longrightarrow 2CO_2 + 3H_2O$$

Tip When balancing alcohol combustion equations, don't forget that the alcohol already contains one oxygen atom. Here you only need three oxygen molecules, not three and a half!

Reaction with sodium

Method: *with care*, add a small piece of sodium to the alcohol in an evaporating basin.

Observation: fizz, as hydrogen is evolved.

Equation: $2C_2H_5OH + 2Na \longrightarrow 2C_2H_5O^-Na^+ + H_2$

The product is sodium **ethoxide** — or in general, the sodium **alkoxide**. Note that the bond between the oxygen and the sodium is ionic and *not* covalent.

Dehydration

Method: pass alcohol vapour over a hot catalyst, such as aluminium oxide.

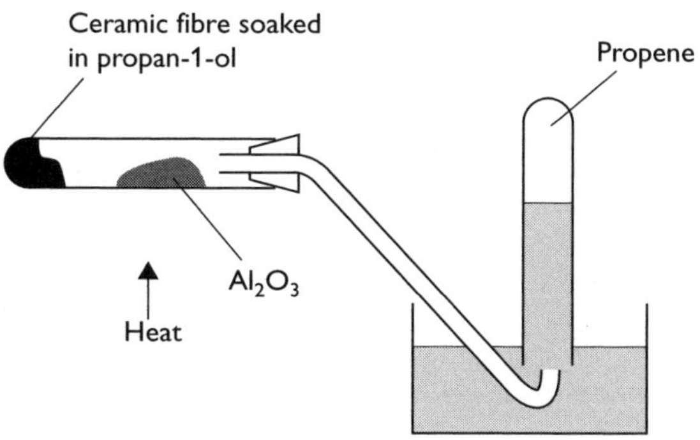

Alternatively, heat the liquid alcohol with concentrated sulphuric or phosphoric acid.

Observation: a gas is given off.

Equation: $CH_3–CH_2–CH_2–OH \longrightarrow CH_3–CH{=}CH_2 + H_2O$
Propan-1-ol → Propene

The –OH group and a hydrogen atom from an adjacent carbon are lost, forming water. The gas given off is the resulting **alkene**. The double bond occurs *next to where the –OH group is lost.* This is called an **elimination** reaction.

Complete oxidation
Method: heat the alcohol *under reflux* with a solution of sodium dichromate in sulphuric acid.

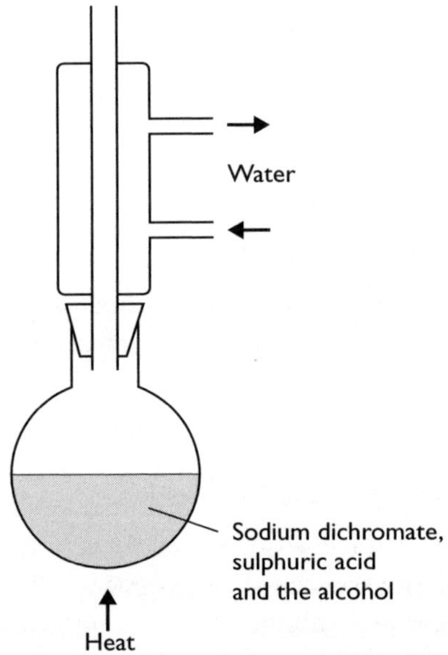

Observation: the sodium dichromate turns from orange to green.

Primary alcohols are oxidised to **carboxylic acids**.

$CH_3–CH_2–CH_2–OH \longrightarrow CH_3–CH_2–COOH$
Propan-1-ol → Propanoic acid

Secondary alcohols are oxidised to **ketones**.

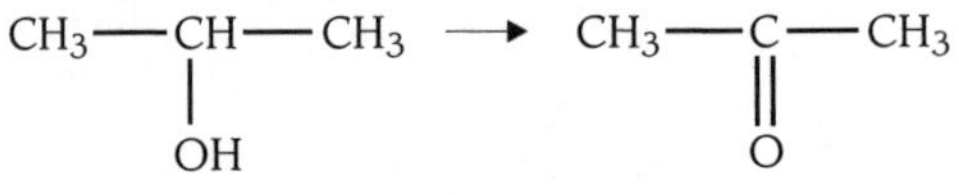

Tertiary alcohols *cannot* be oxidised.

Partial oxidation of primary alcohols
Method: heat the alcohol under *distillation* with a solution of sodium dichromate in sulphuric acid.

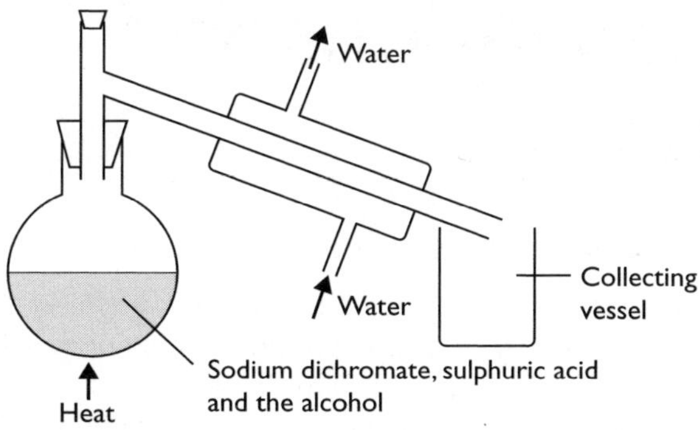

Observation: the sodium dichromate turns from orange to green.

$$\underset{\text{Propan-1-ol}}{CH_3\text{–}CH_2\text{–}CH_2\text{–}OH} \longrightarrow \underset{\text{Propanal}}{CH_3\text{–}CH_2\text{–}CHO}$$

Under these gentle conditions, primary alcohols behave differently and are oxidised to **aldehydes**.

Tip You need to be able to draw the preceding three diagrams.

- It is easier to show connections with bungs than to try to draw quickfit.
- Label the contents of flasks and the heat sources.
- Do not leave 'gaps' in drawings — for instance between the mouth of the flask and the bottom of the condenser.
- Ensure the water connections to a condenser are correctly labelled — in at the lower connection and out at the top.
- Do not draw bungs in the open end of the condenser.

Remember, poor quality diagrams will lose marks!

Aldehydes, ketones and carboxylic acids

Type of compound	Example	Preparation	Test
Aldehyde –CHO 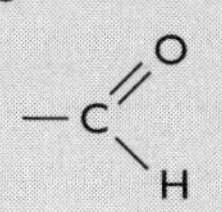	Ethanal CH_3CHO	Heat a primary alcohol under distillation with dilute sulphuric acid/ sodium dichromate	Alkaline Benedict's solution turns from clear blue to a red precipitate No reaction with sodium carbonate solution
Ketone –CO 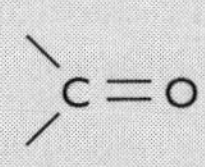	Propanone CH_3COCH_3	Heat a secondary alcohol under reflux with dilute sulphuric acid/sodium dichromate	Stays blue No reaction with sodium carbonate solution
Carboxylic acid $–CO_2H$ 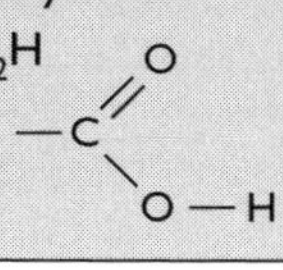	Butanoic acid $C_3H_7CO_2H$	Heat a primary alcohol under reflux with dilute sulphuric acid/sodium dichromate	Stays blue Fizzes with sodium carbonate solution because CO_2 is produced

Mole calculations and equations

Moles of atoms and molecules

The **mole** is the chemist's unit for the amount of 'stuff'. It can apply to anything. You can have a mole of atoms (e.g. 20 g of neon) and a mole of molecules (e.g. 160 g of bromine, Br_2. (Incidentally, 160 g of bromine *molecules*, Br_2, is also *two* moles of bromine *atoms*, Br, because each bromine molecule is made of two bromine atoms.) You can have a mole of an ionic substance (e.g. 58.5 g of sodium chloride), a mole of a covalent compound (e.g. 46 g of ethanol, C_2H_5OH) or even a mole of electrons.

The number of particles in a mole is 600 000 000 000 000 000 000 000 (better written as 6×10^{23}). This number is called the **Avogadro constant**.

To work out the number of moles of something, you need to know its **relative atomic mass** or its **relative formula mass** (sometimes called the relative molecular mass). They are the mass that an atom or molecule, respectively, would have on a scale where an atom of carbon-12 (the common carbon isotope) has a mass of 12.

The relative atomic mass is therefore the number of times one atom of an element is heavier than one-twelfth of an atom of carbon-12.

The relative formula mass is the sum of relative atomic masses making up the formula. For example, for ethanol, C_2H_5OH:

$2 \times$ C atoms $= 2 \times 12 = 24$
$6 \times$ H atoms $= 6 \times 1 = 6$
$1 \times$ O atoms $= 1 \times 16 = 16$
Total $= 46$

Molar mass

This important quantity is the mass of one mole. It is the relative atomic mass (if you are dealing with atoms) or the relative formula mass (if you are dealing with molecules of an element, such as Br_2, or a compound, such as NaCl (ionic) or C_2H_5OH (covalent)). It is expressed in grams per mole ($g\,mol^{-1}$). If you are asked for a molar mass in an exam question, do not forget the units.

Now you are ready to calculate how many moles of 'stuff' you are dealing with. To find the number of moles, you divide the mass you have by the molar mass:

$$\text{number of moles} = \frac{\text{mass in g}}{\text{molar mass}}$$

So, if you have 2.3 g of ethanol, then you have

$$\frac{2.3}{46} = 0.05 \text{ moles}$$

Formulae

These can be worked out from constituent masses by calculating the ratio of moles. Since all moles contain the same number of atoms, this gives the ratio of atoms.

Example 1

A hydrocarbon contains 3.0 g of carbon and 1.0 g of hydrogen. Calculate its formula.

The formula can be worked out like this:

	Carbon	**Hydrogen**
Mass/g	3.0	1.0
Moles	3.0/12 = 0.25	1.0/1 = 1.0
Ratio (divide by smaller)	1	4

Thus the formula is CH_4. This is called the **empirical formula**, since it is the simplest ratio of the atoms. In this case, it is also the **molecular formula** of methane, that is, the actual formula of the molecule.

Example 2

Calculate the formula of a hydrocarbon containing 85.7% carbon.

This can be done in a very similar way, provided it is realised that the remaining 14.3% must be hydrogen. The percentages mean that 85.7 g of carbon combine with 14.3 g of hydrogen.

	Carbon	**Hydrogen**
Mass/g	85.7	14.3
Moles	85.7/12 = 7.14	14.3/1 = 14.3
Ratio (divide by smaller)	1	2

The empirical formula is CH_2. Bonding theory tells us that this is not possible, so we try C_2H_4. This is possible, as are C_3H_6, C_4H_8 and so on. Therefore, CH_2 is the empirical formula of the alkene homologous series.

Example 3

What is the percentage of nitrogen by mass in the fertiliser ammonium nitrate (NH_4NO_3)?

This is virtually the reverse of the previous method.

The relative formula mass of $NH_4NO_3 = 14 + 4 + 14 + 48 = 80$

It contains two nitrogen atoms (= 28)

Thus, % nitrogen $= \frac{28}{80} \times 100 = 35\%$

Equations

These show that atoms are just rearranged in chemical reactions, not created or destroyed. So, equations must *balance* — there must be the same number of each atom on each side. For example, methane burns in oxygen to form carbon dioxide and water. If the formulae of the reactants and products are written as follows:

$$CH_4 + O_2 \longrightarrow CO_2 + H_2O$$

you can see that the equation is not balanced.

We cannot change the formulae of the molecules but we can change the number of moles reacting, that is, the numbers in front of the molecules' formulae. Putting '2' in front of H_2O gives four hydrogens on each side. The carbon atoms are already balanced, so now it is only the oxygens that are unbalanced. Having doubled the water molecules, there are now four oxygen atoms on the right, so we need $2O_2$ on the left to balance:

$$CH_4 + 2O_2 \longrightarrow CO_2 + 2H_2O$$

Sometimes, an odd number of oxygen atoms is needed in these circumstances. Then it is permissible to write the equation as either:

$$2C_3H_7OH + 9O_2 \longrightarrow 6CO_2 + 8H_2O$$

or

$$C_3H_7OH + 4\tfrac{1}{2}O_2 \longrightarrow 3CO_2 + 4H_2O$$

Tip It is permissible to use halves (more so at AS than at GCSE).

State symbols

The **state symbols** are:

- (g) gas
- (l) liquid
- (s) solid
- (aq) aqueous solution

They add more information to an equation. For example:

$$Mg(s) + 2HCl(aq) \longrightarrow MgCl_2(aq) + H_2(g)$$

Tip You need only add state symbols to an equation when the question specifically asks for them. Otherwise it is safest to leave them out.

Types of reaction

You need to be able to recognise the following types of reaction:

- thermal decomposition
- precipitation
- redox

Thermal decomposition

A single reactant is broken down on heating into several different products, for example:

$$CaCO_3(s) \longrightarrow CaO(s) + CO_2(g)$$

Precipitation

A solid product is made by mixing two solutions, for example:

$FeCl_2(aq) + 2NaOH(aq) \longrightarrow Fe(OH)_2(s) + 2NaCl(aq)$

This equation can also be written ionically, missing out the 'spectator' ions, which do not change during the reaction — in this case sodium and chloride.

$Fe^{2+}(aq) + 2OH^-(aq) \longrightarrow Fe(OH)_2(s)$

Redox

Redox reactions involve an element gaining or losing oxygen or changing its ionic charge. For example:

$Fe_2O_3(s) + 3Zn(s) \longrightarrow 2Fe(s) + 3ZnO(s)$

Here, the iron has been reduced because it has *lost* oxygen while the zinc has been oxidised because it has *gained* oxygen.

Oxidation and reduction can also be defined as loss or gain of electrons, as in the example below:

$Fe(s) + Cu^{2+}(aq) \longrightarrow Fe^{2+}(aq) + Cu(s)$

Here, you need to remember **oilrig**. **O**xidation **i**s **l**oss (of electrons) and **r**eduction **i**s **g**ain (of electrons). The iron has become a positive ion by losing two electrons. It has been oxidised. The copper has changed from a positive ion to an uncharged atom. It has gained the two electrons lost by the iron. The copper ion has been reduced.

Tip Practise writing equations for these types of reaction. You need to be able to construct and interpret balanced equations (both full and ionic) including the use of state symbols.

Calculations from equations

The numbers *before* formulae in equations indicate how many moles are reacting.

The rules are:

- Turn the mass of the given substance into moles.
- Use the ratio from the equation to calculate moles of the required substance.
- Turn the moles back to masses.

Example

Calculate the mass of sodium carbonate that is formed when 16.8 g of sodium hydrogen carbonate are heated. (r.a.m. Na, 23; C, 12; H, 1; O, 16)

$2NaHCO_3 \longrightarrow Na_2CO_3 + H_2O + CO_2$

The molar mass of $NaHCO_3 = 23 + 1 + 12 + 48 = 84\,g\,mol^{-1}$

So, moles of $NaHCO_3 = 16.8/84 = 0.20$

The equation shows that 2 moles of $NaHCO_3$ form 1 mole of Na_2CO_3. So 0.20 moles of $NaHCO_3$ will form 0.10 moles of Na_2CO_3. This has a mass of 10.6 g (molar mass of $Na_2CO_3 = (2 \times 23) + 12 + 48 = 106\,g\,mol^{-1}$).

A variation on this question uses the fact that *1 mole of molecules of a gas occupies 24 dm³ at room temperature and pressure* (you will be given this information when you need it).

To calculate the volume of carbon dioxide formed, note that the same numbers of moles of CO_2 as Na_2CO_3 are formed, in this case, 0.10 moles. Thus, $0.10 \times 24 = 2.4\,dm^3$ of CO_2 gas are formed at room temperature and pressure.

If we are dealing with reactants and products that are *all* gases, the volumes are proportional to the moles reacting. Therefore, for the combustion of methane:

$$CH_4(g) + 2O_2(g) \longrightarrow CO_2(g) + 2H_2O(g)$$

Here, one volume of methane (say $1.0\,dm^3$) would react with two volumes ($2.0\,dm^3$) of oxygen to form one volume ($1.0\,dm^3$) of carbon dioxide and two volumes ($2.0\,dm^3$) of water vapour.

Percentage yield

We tend to assume that all reactions produce 100% theoretical yield. However, this is often not the case, especially in organic reactions where side-reactions can lower the yield significantly. You may be asked to calculate the percentage yield of a material.

Example

In an experiment to prepare hexene from hexan-1-ol, 4.00 g of product were obtained from 10.2 g of starting material. Calculate the percentage yield.

$$C_6H_{13}OH \longrightarrow C_6H_{12} + H_2O$$

Hexan-1-ol   Hexene

The molar mass of hexan-1-ol is $102\,g\,mol^{-1}$.

So the number of moles of hexan-1-ol used = 10.2/102 = 0.1 mole.

According to the equation, 1 mole of hexan-1-ol produces 1 mole of hexene. Therefore, 0.1 mole of hexan-1-ol produces 0.1 mole of hexene.

The molar mass of hexene is $84\,g\,mol^{-1}$.

Therefore, the maximum theoretical mass of hexene = $0.1 \times 84 = 8.40$ g.

$$\text{Percentage yield} = \frac{\text{actual yield}}{\text{theoretical yield}} \times 100$$

$$= \frac{4.00}{8.40} \times 100$$

$$= 47.6\%$$

Enthalpy changes

Heat may be given out or absorbed when chemical reactions occur. The stored chemical energy that accounts for this is called **enthalpy**. **Enthalpy level diagrams**, such as those below, illustrate this:

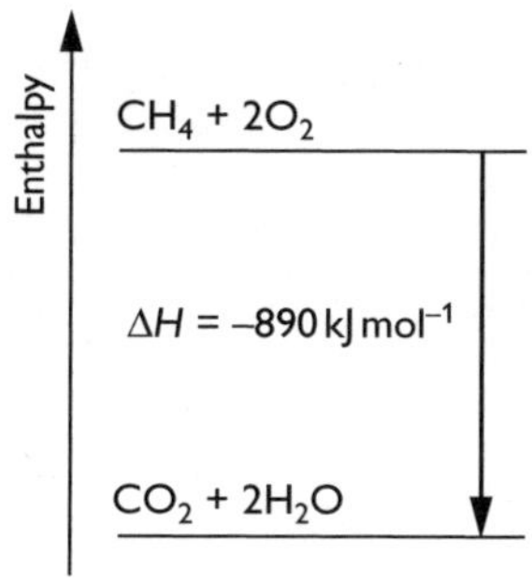

The combustion of methane — **exothermic**

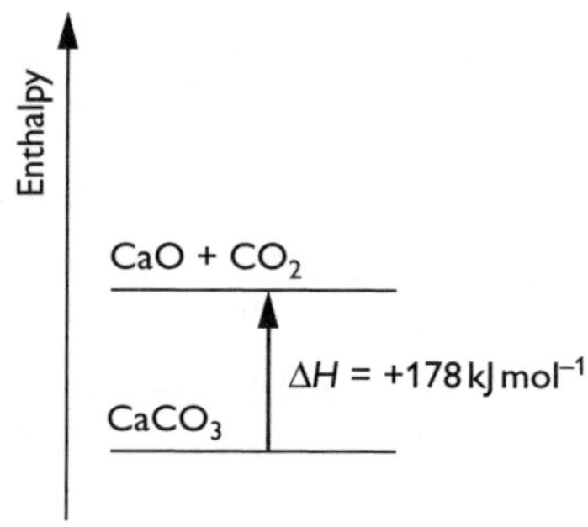

The decomposition of calcium carbonate — **endothermic**

The *change* in enthalpy can be measured directly for some reactions, or indirectly for others by using **cycles**. Enthalpy change has the symbol ΔH.

- When enthalpy is *lost*, ΔH is *negative* and heat is *given out* — an **exothermic** reaction.
- When enthalpy is *gained*, ΔH is *positive* and heat is *taken in* — an **endothermic** reaction.

Measuring enthalpy changes

The enthalpy changes that occur during the combustion of liquid fuels can be measured using the apparatus illustrated below:

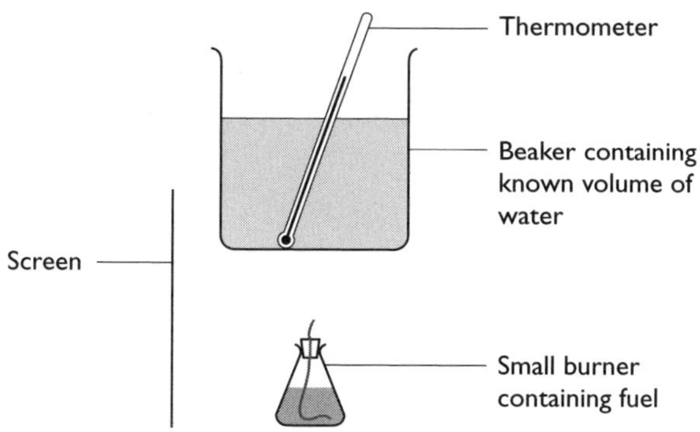

- The intial temperature of a known mass of water is measured.
- The initial mass of the fuel is measured.

- The fuel is ignited and the energy produced heats the water, resulting in a temperature rise.
- The final temperature of the water is recorded and the temperature change calculated.
- The fuel is reweighed to find out how much has been burnt.

The energy produced in **joules** = mass of water × 4.18 × temperature change

The figure 4.18 comes from the fact that it requires 4.18 joules of energy to raise the temperature of 1.00 g of water by 1.00 °C. It is called the specific heat capacity. You will always be given this figure.

$$\text{The moles of fuel burnt} = \frac{\text{mass of fuel burnt}}{\text{molar mass of fuel}}$$

$$\text{The enthalpy change for the combustion of the fuel in } \mathbf{kJ\,mol^{-1}} = \frac{\text{energy produced in joules}}{1000 \times \text{the moles of fuel burnt}}$$

Answers from such experiments are inaccurate because of heat losses to the surroundings and evaporation of the fuel.

Standard enthalpy changes

Enthalpy changes vary with the conditions. **Standard conditions** enable us to compare enthalpy changes. These are defined as:

- a *specified* temperature, usually 298 K
- 1 atmosphere pressure
- a concentration of 1 mol dm^{-3}

All reagents and products are in their normal physical states under these conditions.

Standard enthalpy change is written as $\Delta H^{\ominus}$.

Standard enthalpy change of reaction, $\Delta H^{\ominus}_{r}$, refers to the number of moles shown in the equation, at a pressure of 1 atmosphere, at a temperature of 298 K, with the substances in the physical states (gas, liquid, solid) normal to these conditions.

Standard enthalpy change of formation, $\Delta H^{\ominus}_{f}$, is the enthalpy change that occurs when *1 mole* of a compound (in its *standard state*) is formed from its elements (in their *standard states*) under standard conditions.

$Mg(s) + \frac{1}{2}O_2(g) \longrightarrow MgO(s)$ $\Delta H^{\ominus}_{f} = -601.7\ \text{kJ mol}^{-1}$

Hess's law

Hess's law states that *the enthalpy change in going from reactants to products is independent of the route taken*. This means that however a chemical change is achieved, the overall enthalpy change will always be the same.

Hess cycles are used to measure enthalpy changes indirectly.

Example 1

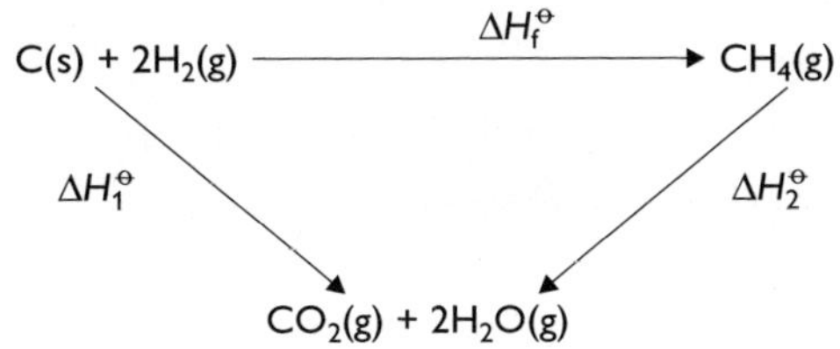

Here $\Delta H_f^\ominus$ is the enthalpy change of formation of CH_4, which cannot be measured directly because hydrogen and carbon do not react to form methane. $\Delta H_1^\ominus$ is the sum of the enthalpy change of formation of carbon dioxide and twice the enthalpy change of formation of water. $\Delta H_2^\ominus$ is the enthalpy change of combustion of methane.

By Hess's law:

$$\Delta H_1^\ominus = \Delta H_f^\ominus + \Delta H_2^\ominus$$

So, $\Delta H_f^\ominus = \Delta H_1^\ominus - \Delta H_2^\ominus$

Example 2

The enthalpy change of a reaction can be measured using enthalpy changes of formation (available in tables).

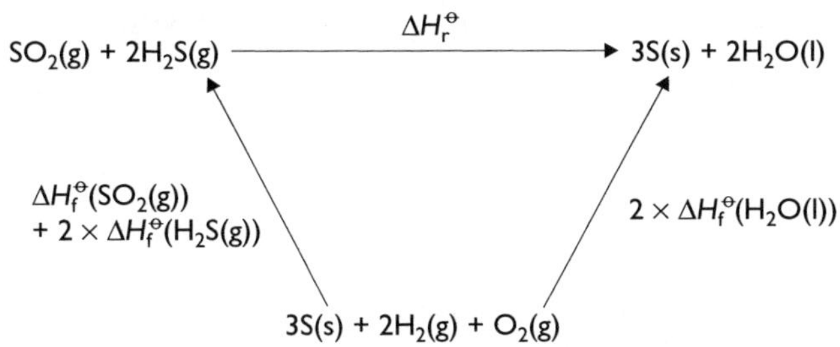

Using Hess's law, follow the arrows round.

The direct route = the sum of the stages in the indirect route:

$$2\Delta H_f^\ominus(H_2O) = (\Delta H_f^\ominus(SO_2) + 2\Delta H_f^\ominus(H_2S)) + \Delta H_r^\ominus$$

Rearranging, we have

$$\Delta H_r^\ominus = -(\Delta H_f^\ominus(SO_2) + 2\Delta H_f^\ominus(H_2S)) + 2\Delta H_f^\ominus(H_2O)$$

Note:

- $\Delta H_f^\ominus$ of an *element* is zero.
- It is necessary to multiply the $\Delta H_f^\ominus$ values of compounds by the number of moles in the equation.

Often a cycle is not asked for. Then the problem in Example 2 can be dealt with by a simpler method. The $\Delta H_f^\ominus$ values in kJ mol^{-1} are:

$$SO_2(g) + 2H_2S(g) \longrightarrow 3S(s) + 2H_2O(l)$$

−297	2 × −21	0	2 × −286

$\Delta H_r^\ominus$ = sum of $\Delta H_f^\ominus$ (products) – sum of $\Delta H_f^\ominus$ (reactants)

Therefore:

$\Delta H_r^\ominus = 2 \times -286 - (-297 + (2 \times -21)) = -233\,\text{kJ mol}^{-1}$

Tip There are many exam questions requiring use of this equation. Practise these calculations.

Acids and bases

Definitions

As our knowledge and understanding of acids and bases have developed, various definitions have arisen. One of the most useful early definitions was that of Arrhenius:

- An acid is a compound that produces H^+ ions in water.
- An alkali is a compound that produces OH^- ions in water.

However, this definition applies to aqueous systems only. A more general definition was needed that could be applied to reactions between gases and to solvents other than water, such as liquid ammonia. Brønsted and Lowry developed such a definition:

- An acid is a proton *donor*.
- A base is a proton *acceptor*.

This is illustrated by the following examples:

$HCl(g) + NH_3(g) \longrightarrow NH_4^+Cl^-(s)$

(Here, the HCl has donated a proton and is therefore an acid. The ammonia has gained a proton and is therefore a base.)

$H_2O(l) + HCl(g) \longrightarrow H_3O^+(aq) + Cl^-(aq)$

(Again, the HCl has donated a proton and is therefore an acid. The water has accepted the proton and is therefore the base. The H_3O^+ ion formed is called the **oxonium** ion.)

Strong and weak acids and bases

Strong and weak acids and bases have nothing to do with 'concentrated' and 'dilute'. You can have a strong acid that is dilute (e.g. dilute hydrochloric acid) and a weak acid that is concentrated (e.g. concentrated ethanoic acid).

A strong acid is one in which every single molecule ionises. In water, 1 mole of HCl produces 1 mole of H^+ ions.

A weak acid is one in which only a small proportion of its molecules ionise. In aqueous solution, 1 mole of ethanoic acid produces only 0.001 moles of H^+ ions.

The same concept applies to bases and the production of OH^- ions.

Titrations

A titration is an accurate method of measuring how much acid reacts with a given amount of alkali (or vice versa).

One of the solutions is a **standard solution** — the concentration is accurately known. Standard solutions are made up in **volumetric flasks**.

- A clean **pipette** — washed with distilled water followed by the solution to be used in it — is used to measure a known volume of standard solution into a conical flask.
- A few drops of indicator are added to the flask.
- The solution of unknown concentration is placed in a clean **burette** — washed with distilled water followed by the solution to be used in it.
- A rough titration is carried out. The solution from the burette is added to the contents of the flask, 1 cm^3 at a time, until the indicator changes colour. The flask is shaken between additions.
- An accurate titration is then carried out. A quantity of solution, 1 cm^3 less than that used in the rough titration, is added from the burette to a new sample of the unknown. Addition is continued one drop at a time, swirling the flask between additions, until the indicator *just* changes colour.
- Further accurate titrations are carried out until two values within 0.1 cm^3 of each other are obtained.
- The average of the values obtained by the accurate titrations is then calculated.

Tip Make sure you know at least one indicator. Phenolphthalein, for instance, is pink in alkali and colourless in acid.

Titration calculations

Titration calculations involve **moles**, **volumes** and **concentrations**, which can be in terms of **mol dm^{-3}** or **g dm^{-3}**.

Example

In a titration to find the solubility of calcium hydroxide, 25.0 cm^3 of saturated calcium hydroxide was pipetted into a conical flask and was titrated with 0.0500 mol dm^{-3} HCl. 15.1 cm^3 of acid were required to neutralise the calcium hydroxide. (This was the average of three accurate titrations.) Calculate the calcium hydroxide concentration.

Find the number of moles in 15.1 cm^3 of 0.0500 M HCl (M means the same as mol dm^{-3}).

Use the formula:

$$\textbf{number of moles} = \frac{\textbf{volume}}{\textbf{1000}} \times \textbf{concentration}$$

$$\text{moles of HCl} = \frac{15.1}{1000} \times 0.0500 = 7.55 \times 10^{-4} \text{ moles HCl}$$

Write the balanced equation:

$Ca(OH)_2 + 2HCl \longrightarrow CaCl_2 + 2H_2O$

Therefore, 2 moles of HCl are needed to react with 1 mole of calcium hydroxide.

$$\text{moles of calcium hydroxide reacted} = \frac{7.55 \times 10^{-4}}{2} = 3.775 \times 10^{-4}$$

This is the number of moles of calcium hydroxide in the original 25.0 cm^3 of saturated solution.

Use the formula **number of moles = (volume/1000)** × **concentration** to find the concentration of the calcium hydroxide:

$$3.775 \times 10^{-4} = \frac{25}{1000} \times M$$

$$M = 3.775 \times 10^{-4} \times \frac{1000}{25} = 0.0151 \text{ mol dm}^{-3}$$

It might be necessary to convert this into $g\,dm^{-3}$. To do this, multiply the answer by the molar mass of the calcium hydroxide (74 $g\,mol^{-1}$):

$0.0151 \times 74 = 1.12\text{ g dm}^{-3}$

Questions & Answers

In this section of the guide, there are 12 questions which between them test all requirements of the Unit 1 specification. They represent the kinds of question you will get in the unit test. Unlike in the real thing, there are no lines or spaces left for the answers. Instead, the presence of a space or number of lines is indicated. The number of marks is, of course, also shown. However, taken together, these questions are much longer than a single paper, so do not try to do them all in 75 minutes.

After each question, you will find the answers of two candidates — Candidate A and Candidate B (using different candidates for each question). In each case, Candidate A is performing at the C/D level, while Candidate B is an A-grade candidate.

Examiner's comments

All candidate responses are followed by examiner's comments. These are preceded by the icon *e* and indicate where credit is due. In the weaker answers, they also point out areas for improvement, specific problems and common errors.

How to use this section

- Do the question, giving yourself a time limit of a minute a mark; do not look at the candidates' answers or examiner's comments before you attempt the question yourself.
- Compare your answers with the candidates' answers and decide what the correct answer is; still do not look at the examiner's comments while doing this.
- Finally, look at the examiner's comments.

Completing this section will teach you a lot of chemistry and vastly improve your exam technique.

Short-answer questions

(1) Zinc reacts with iron(III) chloride solution as shown:

$$Zn(s) + 2FeCl_3(aq) \longrightarrow ZnCl_2(aq) + 2FeCl_2(aq)$$

(a) Write the ionic equation for this reaction. Include state symbols but omit any spectator ions. (*space*) (2 marks)

(b) Has the iron in $FeCl_3$ been oxidised or reduced? Explain your answer. (*2 lines*) (1 mark)

Total: 3 marks

Candidates' answers to Question 1

Candidate A

(a) $Zn(s) + 2Fe^{3+}(aq) \longrightarrow Zn^{2+}(aq) + 2Fe^{2+}(s)$

Candidate B

(a) $Zn(s) + 2Fe^{3+}(aq) \longrightarrow Zn^{2+}(aq) + 2Fe^{2+}(aq)$

e Candidate A has given the correct equation and scores 1 mark. However, the state symbols are wrong — no solid is formed. Candidate B scores both marks.

Candidate A

(b) Reduced, because chlorine has been added.

Candidate B

(b) Reduced, because the ionic charge has gone down by one.

e Candidate A does not score. As the answer is a '50/50' choice, the mark is for the reason, which Candidate B has given correctly.

■ ■ ■

(2) Iron(II) chloride solution reacts with sodium hydroxide solution as shown:

$$FeCl_2(aq) + NaOH(aq) \longrightarrow Fe(OH)_2(s) + NaCl(aq)$$

(a) Write out the balanced equation (*1 line*) (1 mark)

(b) What type of reaction is this? (*1 line*) (1 mark)

Total: 2 marks

Candidates' answers to Question 2

Candidate A

(a) $FeCl_2(aq) + 2NaOH(aq) \longrightarrow Fe(OH)_2(s) + NaCl(aq)$

Candidate B

(a) $FeCl_2(aq) + 2NaOH(aq) \longrightarrow Fe(OH)_2(s) + 2NaCl(aq)$

e Candidate A has left out the second '2' and does not score. Candidate B is correct.

Candidate A

(b) Redox

Candidate B

(b) Precipitation

It is not redox, as the charge on the iron ion stays the same (2+). So Candidate A does not score. Candidate B is correct, for 1 mark. A solid precipitate of iron(II) hydroxide is formed.

■ ■ ■

(3) There are two isomers of C_4H_{10}. One is butane. Draw the displayed formula for the other isomer and give its name. (*space*) (2 marks)

Total: 2 marks

Candidates' answers to Question 3

Candidate A

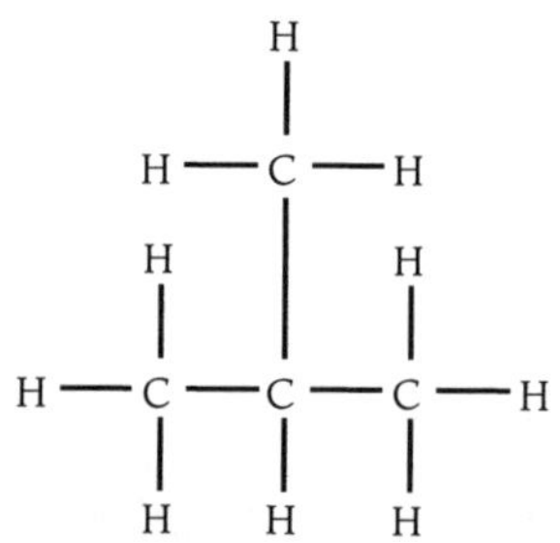

Isopropane

Candidate B

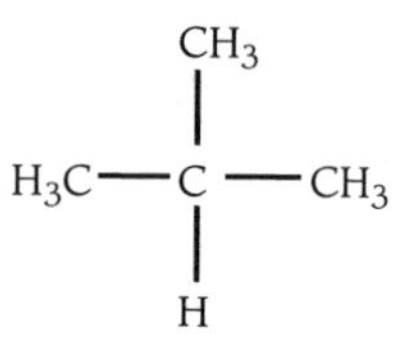

Methylpropane

Candidate A scores 1 mark for the correct displayed formula of the isomer but the name is incorrect. Candidate B has the name correct but she has not fully displayed the structure, so she also scores 1 mark.

■ ■ ■

(4) (a) Give the full electronic configuration of a sodium atom using the *spd* notation. (*1 line*) (1 mark)

(b) The sketch graph shows the first ionisation energies for sodium and magnesium.

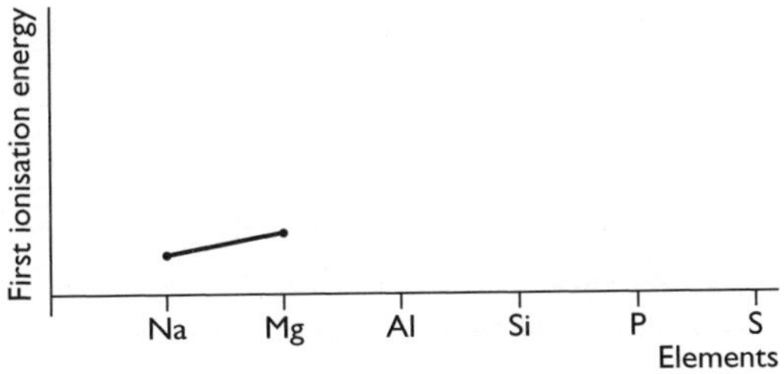

Continue the sketch to show the first ionisation energies for the next four elements of the periodic table. (*space*) (2 marks)

Total: 3 marks

Candidates' answers to Question 4

Candidate A

(a) $3s^1$

Candidate B

(a) $1s^2\ 2s^2\ 2p^6\ 3s^1$

e Candidate A has only given the electron configuration of the outermost sub-shell. The question asks for the full electronic configuration, so Candidate A does not score. Candidate B has the right answer and scores the mark.

Candidate A

(b)

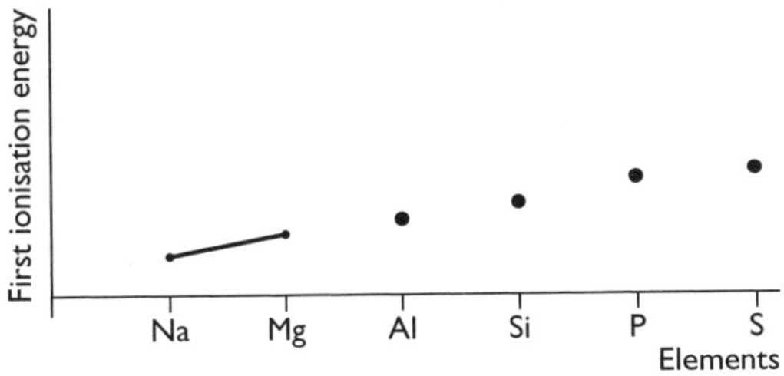

Candidate B

(b)

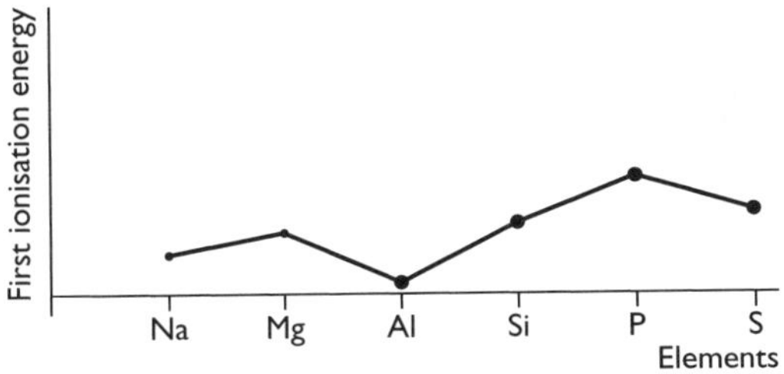

Candidate A scores 1 mark for the gradual rise. However, he fails to get the mark for the drops after magnesium (full *s* sub-shell) and phosphorus (half-full sub-shell). Candidate B scores 1 mark for these drops but does not score the mark for the overall rise in values. The value for aluminium is not below the value for sodium.

■ ■ ■

(5) Candle wax consists of long-chain alkanes which are covalent molecules.

(a) Give the general formula of an alkane with *n* carbon atoms. (*1 line*) (1 mark)

(b) Describe a simple observation that shows that candle wax is a covalent compound. (*1 line*) (1 mark)

Total: 2 marks

Candidates' answers to question 5

Candidate A

(a) C_xH_{2x+2}

Candidate B

(a) C_nH_{2n+2}

Both candidates are correct, for 1 mark.

Candidate A

(b) It will not conduct electricity.

Candidate B

(b) It melts at low temperature.

Candidate A has made a thoughtful point but is not correct because ionic solids do not conduct either! Candidate B's simpler point is correct, for 1 mark.

Overall, Candidate A scores 4 out of 12 marks for the short-answer questions. Candidate B scores 10.

Thermit reaction

(6) When a mixture of aluminium and iron(III) oxide is heated, a very vigorous reaction occurs. This is called the 'thermit' reaction and it gives off a great deal of heat. The equation for the reaction is shown below:

$$Fe_2O_3 + 2Al \longrightarrow Al_2O_3 + 2Fe$$

(a) Explain why iron can be formed by reacting iron(III) oxide with aluminium whereas aluminium cannot be formed by reacting aluminium oxide with iron. (*4 lines*) (2 marks)

(b) State the name given to a reaction that gives out heat. (*1 line*) (1 mark)

(c) (i) Complete the Hess cycle below so that $\Delta H^{\ominus}_{r}$ can be calculated using standard enthalpies of formation. Include state symbols. (2 marks)

$$Fe_2O_3 + 2Al \longrightarrow Al_2O_3 + 2Fe$$

....

(ii) Calculate $\Delta H^{\ominus}_{r}$ for this reaction given that:

$\Delta H^{\ominus}_{f}[Fe_2O_3(s)] = -824.2\ kJ\ mol^{-1}$

$\Delta H^{\ominus}_{f}[Al_2O_3(s)] = -1675.7\ kJ\ mol^{-1}$

Include a sign and units in your answer. (*space*) (2 marks)

(iii) Explain why you do not need values for $\Delta H^{\ominus}_{f}[Fe(s)]$ or $\Delta H^{\ominus}_{f}[Al(s)]$. (*2 lines*) (2 marks)

(d) (i) Name the substance which is being reduced in the thermit reaction. Explain your answer. (*1 line*) (1 mark)

(ii) What type of reaction is the thermit reaction? (*1 line*) (1 mark)

(e) Calculate the mass of aluminium that would react with 80 g of Fe_2O_3. (*space*) (2 marks)

(f) (i) Draw a diagram to show the bonding in a metal such as iron. (*space*) (1 mark)

(ii) Explain how the bonding in metals accounts for their high melting points. (*2 lines*) (1 mark)

(iii) Iron melts at 2081°C. Give one use of iron that depends on its high melting point. (*1 line*) (1 mark)

Total: 16 marks

■ ■ ■

Candidates' answers to Question 6

Candidate A

(a) Aluminium is more reactive than iron.

Candidate B

(a) Aluminium is higher in the reactivity series than iron, so it will reduce iron oxide. Iron, being lower, will not reduce aluminium oxide.

e Candidate A has not said enough to score 2 marks but has made a correct statement worth 1 mark. Candidate B has given a detailed answer to be sure of gaining the second mark. It is sensible to answer such questions 'both ways round', saying why one reaction will occur and why the other won't.

Candidate A

(b) Exothermic or heat-absorbing

Candidate B

(b) Exothermic

e Candidate A has 'hedged her bets'! She has given the right answer followed by a wrong one — 'heat-absorbing' is not correct chemical terminology. She does not score the mark. Candidate B is correct, for 1 mark.

Candidate A

(c) (i) $Fe(s) + Al(s) + O_2(g)$

Candidate B

(c) (i) $2Fe + 2Al + 1\frac{1}{2}O_2$

e Candidate A has given the elements correctly but has not included numbers to balance the equation. However, she has given state symbols and scores the second mark. Candidate B has started well, but has not followed the instruction in the question to give state symbols. He scores 1 mark.

Candidate A

(c) (ii) 851 kJ mol^{-1}

Candidate B

(c) (ii) $\Delta H^{\ominus}_{r} + \Delta H^{\ominus}_{f}(Fe_2O_3) = \Delta H^{\ominus}_{f}(Al_2O_3)$

Therefore $\Delta H^{\ominus}_{r} = -1675.7 + 824.2 = -851$

e Candidate A presumably has the numbers the wrong way round. However, she has not shown her method, so we cannot tell. She scores zero. Candidate B was doing well until he omitted the units (kJ mol^{-1}) from the final answer. He scores 1 mark.

Candidate A

(c) (iii) No data are given.

Candidate B

(c) (iii) They are elements.

e It is true that the lack of data is a hint, but it is not the reason. Candidate A does not score. Candidate B has presumably failed to notice that there are 2 marks available, as his answer is rather short. He should have added that the enthalpy change of formation of an element is always zero, or some alternative wording. He scores 1 of the 2 marks.

Candidate A

(d) (i) Iron

Candidate B

(d) (i) Iron oxide

Candidate A is incorrect. Candidate B scores the mark. The *substance* being reduced is iron oxide.

Candidate A

(d) (ii) Reduction

Candidate B

(d) (ii) Redox

Again, Candidate A fails to score on a matter of exam technique. 'Reduction' is unlikely to be the answer when the word 'reduce' appears in the question. Candidate B has remembered that there is emphasis in the course on classifying reactions as thermal decomposition, precipitation or, as in this case, redox. He scores the mark.

Candidate A

(e) Moles of $Fe_2O_3 = \frac{80}{160} = 0.5$

Therefore, mass of Al = 13.5

Candidate B

(e) Mass of Al $= \frac{80 \times 2 \times 27}{160} = 27\,g$

Candidate A's answer is incorrect and she has not given units. However, she scores 1 mark for showing her working and for working out the moles of iron(III) oxide correctly. Candidate B has not laid out his working so well but scores 2 marks for the correct answer.

Candidate A

(f) (i)

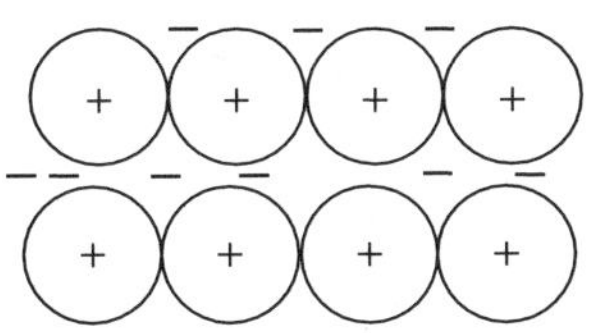

Candidate B

(f) (i)

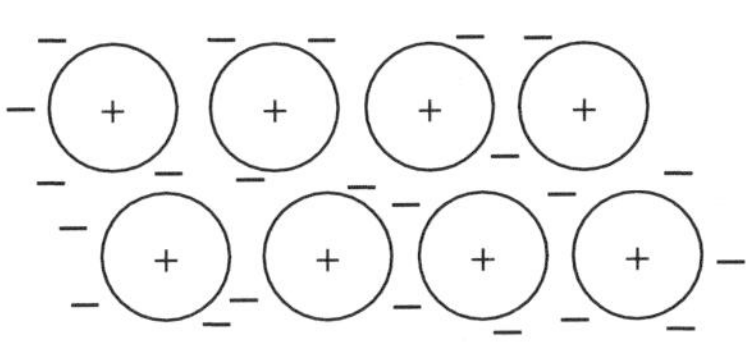

Candidate A has the positive ions touching, so does not score. Candidate B has not checked that the number of plus and minus signs are equal. Examiners penalise large discrepancies here, so he would not score either.

Candidate A

(f) (ii) The atoms are close together.

Candidate B

(f) (ii) There are strong forces between ions and electrons.

e Candidate A has not focused on the word 'bonding' in the question and does not score. Candidate B has, and scores the mark.

Candidate A

(f) (iii) Cylinder blocks for cars

Candidate B

(f) (iii) Bridges

e Candidate A has gone for a use where the structure will have to operate at high temperatures and therefore scores the mark. Candidate B has given an important use of iron but not one where it is heated above 1000 °C, so he does not score.

e **Overall, Candidate A scores 4 out of 16 marks. Candidate B scores 11.**

Atoms and ions of potassium

(7) (a) Potassium has two main isotopes, with the following percentage abundances:

$^{39}_{19}K$, 93.23%

$^{41}_{19}K$, 6.77%

(i) Use this information to work out the molar mass of potassium to four significant figures. Show your working clearly and include units in your answer. (*space*) (2 marks)

(ii) Name the instrument used to measure isotopic abundance. (*1 line*) (1 mark)

(b) State the number of protons, neutrons and electrons in the potassium ion, $^{41}_{19}K^+$. (*1 line*) (3 marks)

(c) (i) Give the electron configuration of a potassium atom, using *s p d* notation. (*1 line*) (1 mark)

(ii) Write an equation to represent the *second* ionisation energy of potassium. Include state symbols in the equation. (*space*) (2 marks)

(iii) Using the axes below, sketch a graph to show the first three ionisation energies of potassium. (2 marks)

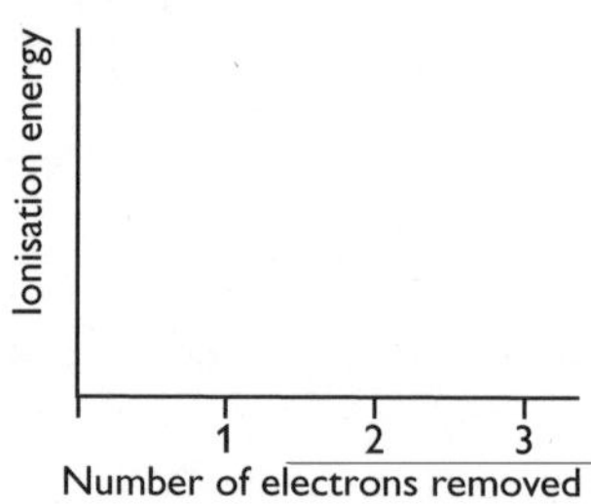

(iv) Would you expect potassium to have a larger or smaller *second* ionisation energy than calcium? Justify your answer. (*2 lines*) (2 marks)

Total: 13 marks

■ ■ ■

Candidates' answers to Question 7

Candidate A

(a) (i) $\frac{(93.23 \times 39) + (6.77 \times 41)}{100} = 39.1354\,\text{g mol}^{-1}$

Candidate B

(a) (i) $(0.9323 \times 39) + (0.0677 \times 41) = 39.14$

Both candidates have the right idea. They fall down on the detail. Candidate A has confused significant figures with decimal places, though he has given the correct units for 'molar mass'. Candidate B has failed to give the units but has the correct number of significant figures. They both score 1 out of 2 marks.

Candidate A

(a) (ii) Spectrometer

Candidate B

(a) (ii) Mass spectrometer

Candidate A has not been specific enough and does not score. Candidate B is correct, for 1 mark.

Candidate A

(b) Protons, 19; neutrons, 20; electrons, 19

Candidate B

(b) Protons, 19; neutrons, 22; electrons, 18

Candidate A scores 1 mark for the correct number of protons. He then gets the number of neutrons confused with the other isotope's neutrons (read the question!). He gives the number of electrons for the atom, not the 1+ ion. Candidate B is correct and scores all 3 marks.

Candidate A

(c) (i) 2,8,8,1

Candidate B

(c) (i) $1s^2\ 2s^2\ 2p^6\ 3s^2\ 3p^6\ 4s^1$

Candidate A has not read the question carefully and has given the electron arrangement by shells. He does not score. Candidate B is correct and scores the mark.

Candidate A

(c) (ii) $K(s) \longrightarrow K^{2+}(g) + 2e^-$

Candidate B

(c) (ii) $K^+(g) \longrightarrow K^{2+}(g) + e^-$

Candidate A has given an incorrect equation for the *second* ionisation energy, which should start from K^+, so he does not score. The state symbols are also wrong — they should all be gases, so he loses the second mark too. Candidate B is correct and scores both marks.

Candidate A

(c) (iii)

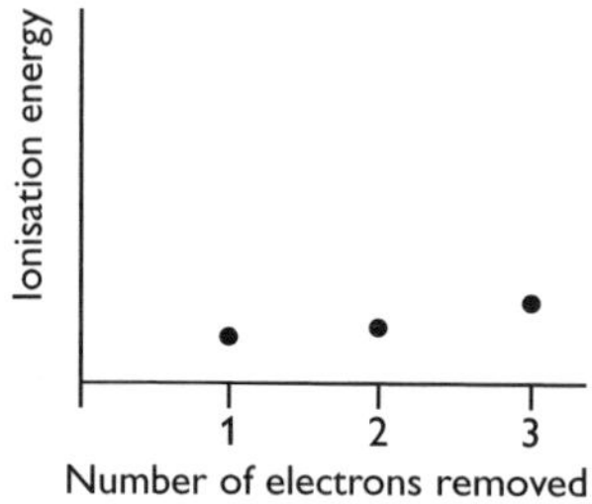

Candidate B

(c) (iii)

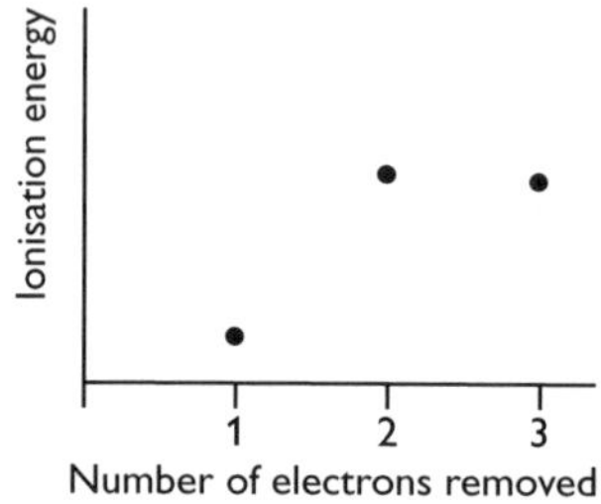

Candidate A scores 1 mark for showing a rise in the successive ionisation energies. However, he has missed the large jump from the first to the second, which occurs because a new shell is being broken into. Candidate B shows this jump but not the overall rise, so she also scores 1 out of 2 marks. A correct sketch would be as follows:

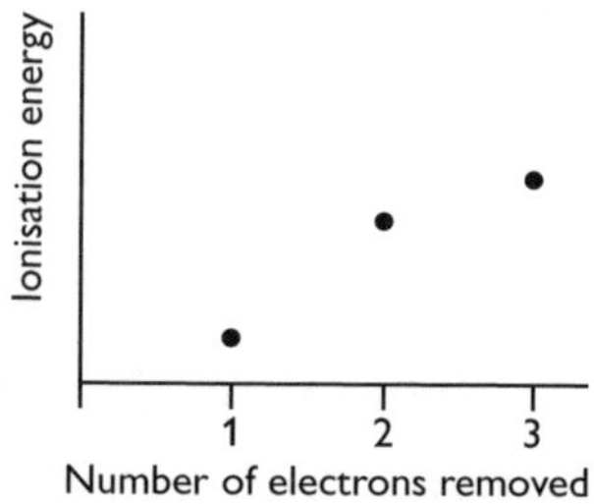

Candidate A

(c) (iv) Smaller, because the electrons are in the same shell but are being removed against the attraction of fewer protons.

Candidate B

(c) (iv) Much larger, because a new shell is being broken into when potassium loses its second electron.

Candidate A gives an answer that is often correct for questions about ionisation energies across a period. However, he shows his error by saying 'the same shell' and he does not score. The second electron to be removed from potassium is in a new shell. Candidate B's answer is correct and she scores 2 marks.

Overall, Candidate A scores 3 marks out of 13. Candidate B scores 11.

Potassium and chlorine

(8) (a) Potassium compounds have a characteristic flame colour.

(i) Describe how you would carry out a flame test to show this colour. (*6 lines*) (3 marks)

(ii) What flame colour would you expect to see? (*1 line*) (1 mark)

(b) The flame colour is given by the most intense line in the emission spectrum of potassium.

(i) Explain how a line in an emission spectrum arises. (*4 lines*) (2 marks)

(ii) Why are there several lines in an emission spectrum? (*2 lines*) (1 mark)

(c) Potassium reacts with chlorine to form an ionic compound.

(i) Describe one piece of evidence indicating that potassium chloride consists of ions. (*3 lines*) (2 marks)

(ii) Draw a 'dot-and-cross' diagram for a chloride ion. Show outer-shell electrons only and the charge on the ion. (*space*) (2 marks)

(iii) Potassium ions and chloride ions have the same number of electrons, yet chloride ions are larger than potassium ions. Suggest a reason for this. (*2 lines*) (2 marks)

(d) Potassium is in group 1; chlorine is in group 7. Describe, in general terms, how the melting point of the element varies as a period is traversed from group 1 to group 7. (*2 lines*) (2 marks)

Total: 15 marks

Candidates' answers to Question 8

Candidate A

(a) (i) The wire is dipped in the compound and then placed in a Bunsen flame.

Candidate B

(a) (i) A nichrome wire is dipped into hydrochloric acid, then the powder, then a flame.

e Candidate A is so vague that she does not score at all. The first mark is for the type of wire (nichrome or platinum), or something simpler like a wet splint. The second mark is for using concentrated hydrochloric acid and the third for the sequence: dip in acid, then dip in powder, then flame. So Candidate B scores the first and third marks but not the second because he did not specify that concentrated acid was needed.

Candidate A

(a) (ii) Purple

Candidate B

(a) (ii) Lilac

e Both answers are acceptable descriptions of the colour and score the mark.

Candidate A

(b) (i) Electrons fall down between energy levels, giving out light.

Candidate B

(b) (i) Electrons are excited to higher energy levels. When they drop back they give out light of a specific frequency.

e Candidate A has not described the full process of excitement followed by falling back and scores 1 mark only. Candidate B scores 2 marks.

Candidate A

(b) (ii) Electrons fall different distances.

Candidate B

(b) (ii) There are many energy levels in an atom.

e Candidate A is quite close but is not specific enough. She does not score. Candidate B gives a better answer and scores the mark.

Candidate A

(c) (i) It has a high melting point.

Candidate B

(c) (i) It conducts electricity when it is melted.

e Candidate A has a point. The strong forces between ions lead to a high melting point. However, there are other structures (giant covalent, for example) which have high melting points, so her answer is not specific enough and only scores 1 mark. Candidate B has given a much safer answer, which gains both marks.

Candidate A

(c) (ii)

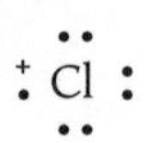

Candidate B

(c) (ii)

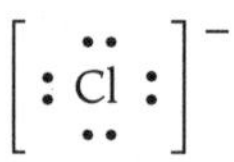

e Candidate A scores 1 mark for showing eight outer electrons in the chloride ion. However, she has not shown the charge on the ion, which was specifically requested in the question. Candidate B scores both marks. Having all dots around the chlorine is acceptable, though it is better practice to show seven dots and one cross as Candidate A has. This shows that one electron comes from elsewhere (e.g. a potassium atom).

Candidate A

(c) (iii) In chloride ions, the electrons repel more; that is why they are large.

Candidate B

(c) (iii) Potassium has more protons pulling the electrons in more tightly.

Candidate A is wrong and does not score. The question says they both have the same number of electrons — hence the repulsion is the same. Candidate B scores 1 mark for the important point he makes. However, he fails to state that the electrons being pulled in by the protons are all in the outer shell, and so misses the second mark.

Candidate A

(d) It goes up to a peak in the middle of the period.

Candidate B

(d) It rises, then falls.

Both candidates are correct and score 2 marks.

Overall, Candidate A scores 6 marks out of 15. Candidate B scores 13.

Structural isomers of C_3H_8O

(9) (a) Explain what you understand by the term 'structural isomers'. (*2 lines*) (2 marks)

(b) One isomer of C_3H_8O is an alcohol with the following structure:

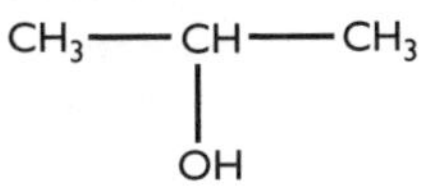

(i) Name this compound. (*1 line*) (1 mark)

(ii) Classify this alcohol as primary, secondary or tertiary. (*1 line*) (1 mark)

(iii) What is the molecular formula of the next member of the homologous series of alcohols? (*1 line*) (1 mark)

(c) The alcohol from (b) can be fully oxidised to a ketone.

(i) Name the *two* reagents needed for this oxidation. (*2 lines*) (2 marks)

(ii) What colour change would you observe as the reaction takes place? (*1 line*) (2 marks)

(iii) Draw a fully labelled diagram of the apparatus you would use for the oxidation. (*space*) (4 marks)

(iv) Give the name and structural formula of the ketone formed by the oxidation of the alcohol. (*space*) (2 marks)

(v) Describe what you would see (if anything) if this ketone were warmed with Benedict's solution. (*1 line*) (1 mark)

(vi) In an experiment, 20.1 g of the ketone was formed from 37.0 g of the alcohol. Calculate the percentage yield. (*space*) (2 marks)

Total: 18 marks

Candidates' answers to Question 9

Candidate A

(a) They have the same formula, but different structures.

Candidate B

(a) Same molecular formula, different structural formulae

Candidate A scores 1 mark for 'different structures' but misses a mark by not putting 'same molecular formula'. Candidate B, though brief, scores the 2 marks.

Candidate A

(b) (i) Propanol

Candidate B

(b) (i) Propan-2-ol

Candidate A's answer is not accurate enough because both propan-1-ol and propan-2-ol exist. He does not score. Candidate B is correct, for 1 mark.

Candidate A

(b) (ii) Secondary

Candidate B

(b) (ii) Tertiary

Candidate A has given the correct answer, for 1 mark. Candidate B has missed the fact that there is a hydrogen atom on the carbon with the –OH group. She does not score.

Candidate A

(b) (iii) C_4H_9OH

Candidate B

(b) (iii) $C_4H_{10}O$

Candidate A is so nearly right, but he does not score the mark. Molecular formulae do not indicate functional groups; they have all atoms of the same type grouped together. Candidate B is correct, for 1 mark.

Candidate A

(c) (i) Potassium dichromate and acid

Candidate B

(c) (i) Sodium dichromate and sulphuric acid

Candidate A has not answered the question carefully enough. 'Acid' is not the name of a reagent, so he scores 1 mark for the first part of his answer only. Candidate B gives the names of two appropriate substances and gains 2 marks.

Candidate A

(c) (ii) Yellow to green

Candidate B

(c) (ii) Orange to green

Candidate A is not careful enough. Dichromates are orange, not yellow. He gains 1 mark for 'green'. Candidate B gains both marks.

Candidate A

(c) (iii)

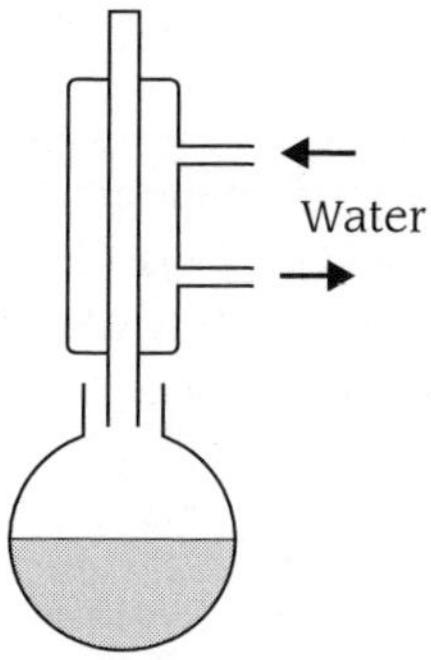

Candidate B

(c) (iii)

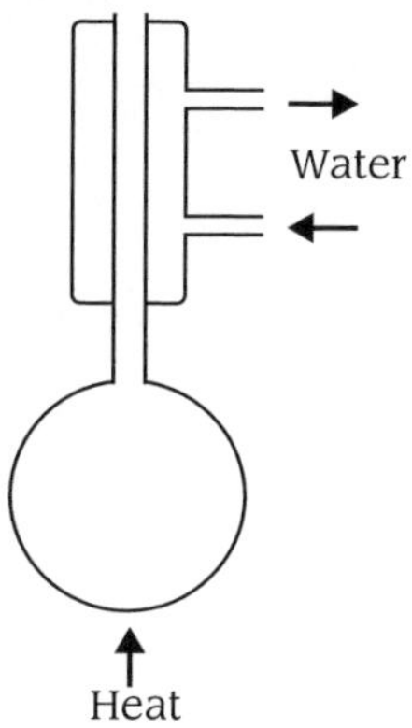

Neither candidate scores full marks for this relatively simple diagram. Candidate A scores for the flask and contents. Candidate B does not — she shows an empty flask! Both score for the reflux condenser but only Candidate B scores for the correct water connections. (Water comes in at the bottom so that it fills the condenser and just a gentle flow can be used.) Candidate B scores for showing heat, which Candidate A does not. Thus, at this point Candidate A has 2 marks and Candidate B has 3. However, there are also penalties in the mark scheme! One is for a poor diagram and both candidates lose this mark — Candidate A has not joined the flask to the condenser with a bung and Candidate B has not shown the flask separate from the condenser. Candidate A has apparently shown a sealed diagram, losing another mark. So, overall, Candidate A does not score and Candidate B scores 2 marks.

Candidate A

(c) (iv) Propanone

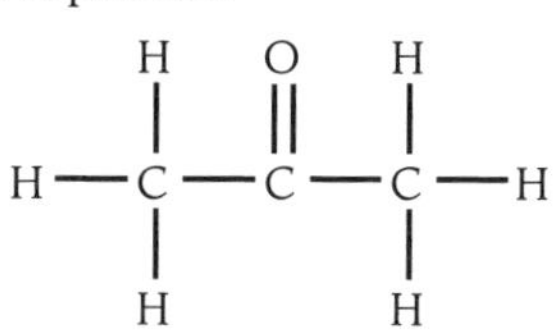

Candidate B

(c) (iv) Propan-2-one

CH_3COCH_3

These answers look rather different but they both score 2 marks. Candidate A has drawn a displayed formula when just a structural formula was asked for. This is all right this way round — but not the other way round when a displayed formula is asked for! There is only one propanone, so Candidate A has the better answer. However, propan-2-one would also be accepted.

Candidate A

(c) (v) Nothing

Candidate B

(c) (v) Stays blue

Candidate A has not quite answered the question. You see a colour, not nothing. Candidate B is correct, for 1 mark.

Candidate A

(c) (vi) $\dfrac{20.1 \times 100}{37} = 54.324\%$

Candidate B

(c) (vi) r.m.m. ketone = 58

r.m.m. alcohol = 50

$$\text{Moles ketone} = \frac{20.1}{58} = 0.347$$

$$\text{Moles alcohol} = \frac{37}{50} = 0.74$$

$$\%\ \text{yield} = \frac{0.347 \times 100}{0.74}$$

$$= 46.9\%$$

Candidate A does not understand what percentage yield means! It is necessary to calculate the amounts (in moles) of ketone and alcohol, since 1 mole of alcohol gives 1 mole of ketone at 100% yield. Candidate A does not score. Even if the calculation were correct, he would have lost the final mark for failing to give his answer to the appropriate number of significant figures — three, since the data are given to three figures. Candidate B has also made a mistake. The answer is 56.2%. She has laid out her answer well so her method can be followed. Can you see where she went wrong? She has calculated the molar mass of the alcohol as 50 and not 60! She loses 1 mark but gains the other because her subsequent working is clear and correct and she has given the answer to three significant figures. This is an example of 'error carried forward', which examiners are keen to use if they can. Candidate B's answer with no working would have scored no marks.

Overall, Candidate A scores 6 marks out of 18. Candidate B scores 14.

Alcohols

(10) An alcohol with formula $CH_3CH_2CH_2CH_2OH$ can be oxidised to an aldehyde using acidified potassium dichromate. Further oxidation also occurs to give an acidic compound.

(a) (i) Give the name and displayed formula of the aldehyde formed. (*space*) (2 marks)

(ii) Name the functional group in the acidic compound formed by further oxidation. (*1 line*) (1 mark)

(iii) State the practical procedure you would use to oxidise the alcohol to the aldehyde, without further oxidation occurring. (*1 line*) (1 mark)

(b) The alcohol can be converted to an alkene.

(i) Name and give the structural formula of the alkene. (*space*) (2 marks)

(ii) Draw a fully labelled diagram of the laboratory apparatus, including the chemicals that you would use, to carry out this reaction and to collect the gas. (*space*) (4 marks)

(iii) Give two names that describe this type of reaction. (*2 lines*) (2 marks)

(c) Another alcohol of formula C_4H_9OH cannot be oxidised using acidified potassium dichromate.

(i) Describe a test for the –OH functional group to which this alcohol will give a positive reaction. Give the result. (*2 lines*) (2 marks)

(ii) Give the structural formula for this alcohol and name it. (*space*) (2 marks)

Total: 16 marks

Candidates' answers to Question 10

Candidate A

(a) (i) Butanal

$CH_3CH_2CH_2COH$

Candidate B

(a) (i) Butan-1-one

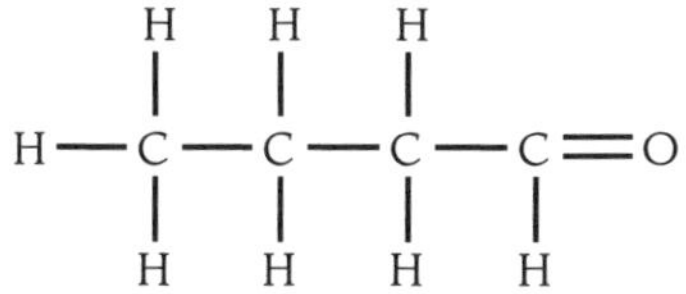

Candidate A has made a mess of the formula, though the name is correct. Aldehydes are written 'CHO' to try to prevent Candidate A's mistake, but to no avail here. She has not given a displayed formula, so does not score. Candidate B has the correct formula, but the name is wrong. When the C=O is on the end carbon, the compound is called an aldehyde, not a ketone. Both candidates score 1 mark.

Candidate A

(a) (ii) Acid

Candidate B

(a) (ii) Carboxylic acid

Candidate A has not given enough detail and does not score. 'Acid' is unlikely to be the answer, as it virtually repeats the question. Candidate B scores the mark.

Candidate A

(a) (iii) Heat with acid dichromate

Candidate B

(a) (iii) Distil

Candidate A has not made the important point that distillation is needed to give the best yield of an aldehyde. Candidate B has written just 'distil'. Does he score the mark without the reagents? Yes, because the reagents are mentioned in the stem of the question.

Candidate A

(b) (i) Butene
$CH_3CH_2CH_2CH_2$

Candidate B

(b) (i) But-1-ene
$CH_3\text{–}CH_2\text{–}CH\text{=}CH_2$

Candidate A does not score, though she is close. Butene is not a unique name because both but-1-ene and but-2-ene exist. Her formula is not acceptable as she has two hydrogen atoms on the second carbon from the right, rather than just one. It is much safer to write structural formulae in the way Candidate B has. He scores both marks.

Candidate A

(b) (ii)

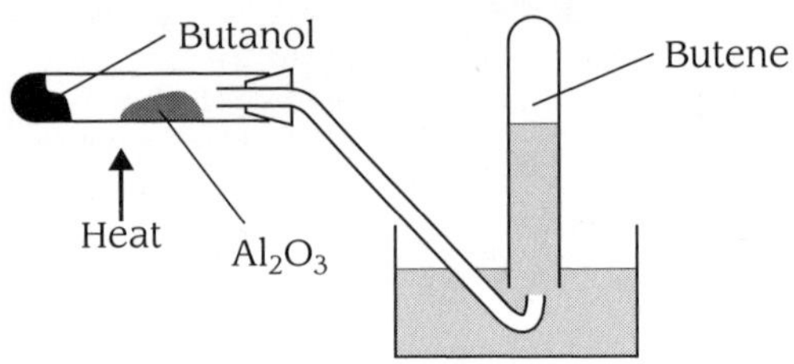

Candidate B

(b) (ii)

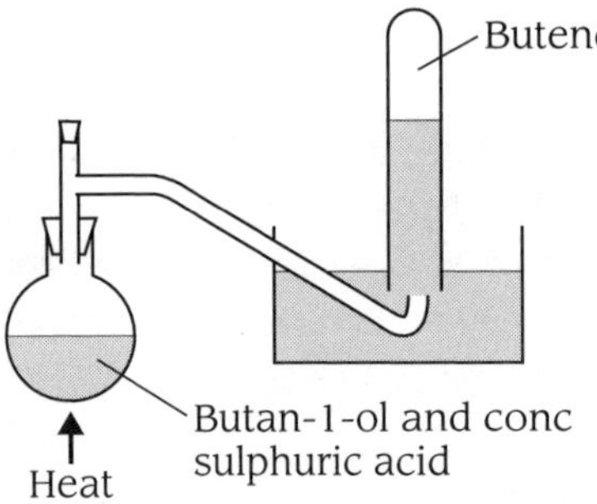

e The candidates have chosen different methods that are both basically correct. Candidate A gains a mark for Al_2O_3 and another mark for collection over water. However, she has not labelled the support for the butanol (e.g. ceramic fibre). The main thing to be heated is the Al_2O_3, so the arrow should be shown there. She scores 2 marks. There are no marks lost for unsealed apparatus or poor diagram. Candidate B scores a mark for the flask containing butanol and one more for concentrated sulphuric acid. He gains another mark for the heat source and a fourth mark for collection over water. However, he loses a mark for a poor diagram (the tube going through the trough). Overall, he scores 3 marks.

Candidate A

(b) (iii) Dehydration; decomposition

Candidate B

(b) (iii) Dehydration; elimination

e Candidate A falls foul of the need to be more specific about decomposition. *Thermal* decomposition must always be stated. However, she gains a mark for dehydration. Candidate B gains both marks.

Candidate A

(c) (i) Decolorises acid permanganate

Candidate B

(c) (i) Reacts with sodium

e Candidate A has failed to understand that this compound is a tertiary alcohol which cannot be oxidised, so she does not score. Candidate B has given the right reaction but he has not provided enough detail for the second mark which is, as always, for the *result* of the test — here 'a fizz' or 'hydrogen evolved'.

Candidate A

(c) (ii) $(CH_3)_3COH$

2-methylpropanol

Candidate B

(c) (ii)

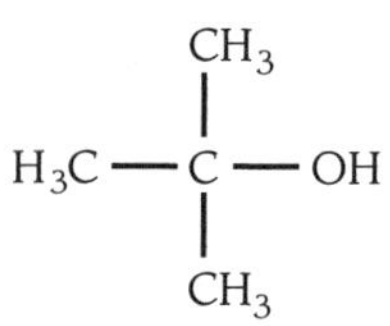

Methylpropan-2-ol

e Both candidates have given acceptable structural formulae for the tertiary alcohol. Candidate B's answer is 'safer', as it makes it less easy to make a mistake. Candidate A does not score a mark for the name as 2-methylpropan-1-ol also exists and must be distinguished from this compound. Candidate B scores the second mark, since the '2' before the -methyl is not essential.

e **Overall, Candidate A scores 5 marks out of 16. Candidate B scores 13.**

Calcium hydroxide

(11) Calcium hydroxide is used by farmers to neutralise the acidity in soil.

(a) Calcium hydroxide is not very soluble in water. A saturated solution of calcium hydroxide was titrated with hydrochloric acid.

$$Ca(OH)_2(aq) + 2HCl(aq) \longrightarrow CaCl_2(aq) + H_2O(l)$$

(i) 10.0 cm^3 of saturated calcium hydroxide solution was measured into a flask for the titration. Give the name of the piece of apparatus that would be used to measure out this volume. (*1 line*) (1 mark)

(ii) Describe the steps you would carry out to obtain one accurate result in a titration, given that you know that the result is approximately 10 cm^3. (*5 lines*) (4 marks)

(iii) The mean result of several accurate titrations is 10.2 cm^3 of 0.0300 mol dm^{-3} hydrochloric acid. Calculate the concentration of the saturated calcium hydroxide solution. (*space*) (3 marks)

(b) Hydrochloric acid is described as a strong acid. Explain what is meant by a strong acid. (*2 lines*) (1 mark)

(c) (i) Using the information in (a) (iii), describe how you would make a colourless, neutral solution of calcium chloride. (*2 lines*) (2 marks)

(ii) Describe how you would obtain pure, dry crystals of calcium chloride from the solution in (c) (i). (*8 lines*) (4 marks)

Total: 15 marks

Candidates' answers to Question 11

Candidate A

(a) (i) Measuring cylinder

Candidate B

(a) (i) Pipette

e Candidate A has not realised the accuracy required. Measuring cylinders measure to an accuracy of ± 1 cm^3 only. 10.0 cm^3 must be measured with a pipette. Candidate B scores the mark.

Candidate A

(a) (ii) Place the acid in the burette. Measure out 10 cm^3 of calcium hydroxide into a conical flask. Titrate the acid into the hydroxide (using indicator) until a change is seen. Repeat several times until a consistent result is obtained.

Candidate B

(a) (ii) Add indicator. Run in the acid until 9 cm^3 have been added. Then proceed slowly until the reaction is finished.

Candidate A has not read the question carefully and considered what is required. He has repeated many of the steps already given in the question (acid in the burette, calcium hydroxide in the flask) and failed to notice that the question asks for just *one* accurate titration. He scores 1 mark for 'using indicator'. Candidate B has remembered the indicator, for which she scores 1 mark. However, she has not made it clear that the titration is continued until a *colour* change is *just* seen. She scores another mark for adding the bulk of the acid quickly. Other marks were available for 'adding the acid drop by drop' (she was too vague here) and 'swirling the flask'.

Candidate A

(a) (iii) $Ca(OH)_2 = 10.2 \times 0.03 \div 10 = 0.0306\,mol\,dm^{-3}$

Candidate B

(a) (iii) Moles $Ca(OH)_2 = \dfrac{10.2 \times 0.03}{2} \div 1000 = 1.53 \times 10^{-4}$

$$\text{Concentration} = \frac{1.53 \times 10^{-4} \times 1000}{10} = 1.53 \times 10^{-2}$$

Candidate A's answer is incorrect and he has shown very little working. Luckily the examiner can see that he has forgotten the 1:2 ratio. As this is his only error, he scores 2 marks. Candidate B has the correct numerical answer, but she loses a mark by not including the units — presumably through carelessness. She scores 2 marks.

Candidate A

(b) It has a high concentration of H^+ ions.

Candidate B

(b) It ionises completely in water.

Candidate A is confusing strength with concentration. Hydrochloric acid is always strong, whatever its concentration, because it dissociates completely in water (rather than reaching an equilibrium). Thus, Candidate A does not score the mark whereas Candidate B does.

Candidate A

(c) (i) Add equal volumes of hydrochloric acid and calcium hydroxide.

Candidate B

(c) (i) Mix $10.2\,cm^3$ of $0.03\,mol\,dm^{-3}$ hydrochloric acid with $10.0\,cm^3$ of saturated calcium hydroxide solution. Do not add indicator.

Candidate A has not worked out what the question requires and does not score. He has not given the concentrations of the solutions being used. The evidence from **(a) (iii)** indicates that the solutions do not react in equal volumes. Candidate B has the right answer, mixing the required amounts in the absence of indicator, which would colour the solution. She scores 2 marks.

Candidate A

(c) (ii) Leave the solution to crystallise. Filter and wash the crystals well with water. Dry.

Candidate B

(c) (ii) Heat the solution to reduce the volume. Cool. Filter. Dry in an oven.

There are four steps here, as Candidate B indicates. Candidate A misses the first mark but scores the second. He loses the third mark because washing the product on the filter would dissolve it. He fails to specify a method for drying the crystals, so he scores 1 mark overall. Meanwhile, Candidate B is steadily scoring the marks. However, she lets herself down at the end by overheating the crystals in an oven. This would drive off the water of crystallisation. Drying between filter papers is the best method. Candidate B scores 3 marks.

Overall, Candidate A scores 4 marks out of 15. Candidate B scores 11.

Barium compounds

(12) (a) The reaction between barium hydroxide and hydrochloric acid is exothermic. 8.55 g of barium hydroxide is added to 40.0 cm^3 of 5.0 mol dm^{-3} HCl. The temperature rises by 34.0 °C.

(i) Calculate the number of moles of calcium hydroxide and of hydrochloric acid. Show that the hydrochloric acid is in excess. (*space*) (3 marks)

(ii) Calculate the energy change using the relationship:

energy change = 4.18 × volume of solution × temperature change

(*space*) (2 marks)

(iii) Use your answer to (i) and (ii) to calculate the standard enthalpy change of the reaction. Remember to include a sign and units in your answer, which should be given to an appropriate number of significant figures. (*space*) (2 marks)

(iv) Describe a suitable piece of apparatus in which to carry out this experiment. Justify your answer. (*2 lines*) (2 marks)

(b) Barium is a member of group 2 of the periodic table. Use your knowledge of the chemical and physical properties of the group 2 elements magnesium to barium to answer the following.

(i) Which has the largest atoms? Justify your answer. (*2 lines*) (2 marks)

(ii) Which reacts most vigorously with water? (*1 line*) (1 mark)

(iii) Which has the carbonate that decomposes at the lowest temperature? (*1 line*) (1 mark)

(c) When barium nitrate is heated, the following reaction takes place:

$$2Ba(NO_3)_2(s) \longrightarrow 2BaO(s) + 4NO_2(g) + O_2(g)$$

(i) What type of reaction is this? (*1 line*) (1 mark)

(ii) Describe what you would expect to see when barium nitrate is heated. Justify your answer. (*2 lines*) (2 marks)

(iii) Nitrogen dioxide is soluble in water. Suggest a simple method for collecting the oxygen from this experiment, uncontaminated with nitrogen dioxide. (*2 lines*) (1 mark)

(iv) What volume of oxygen (at room temperature and pressure) would be produced if 13 g of barium nitrate were decomposed? (Molar volume is 24 $dm^3 mol^{-1}$ at room temperature and pressure.) (*space*) (2 marks)

Total: 19 marks

■ ■ ■

Candidates' answers to Question 12

Candidate A

(a) (i) Moles $Ba(OH)_2 = \frac{8.55}{171} = 0.05$

Moles HCl $= \frac{40 \times 5}{1000} = 0.2$

This is larger than 0.05, hence an excess.

Candidate B

(a) (i) Moles $Ba(OH)_2$ = 0.05. This would require 0.1 mol of HCl, which would be 20 cm^3. Thus the HCl is in excess.

e Candidate A has set out her working well, so it is clear what she is doing. She scores the first 2 marks for the moles of each reagent. Unfortunately, she fails to spot the 2:1 ratio in which they combine, so she does not score the third mark. Candidate B has not answered the part of the question requiring him to calculate the moles of HCl. However, he has calculated the moles of $Ba(OH)_2$ correctly and shown that there is an excess of HCl, so he too scores 2 marks.

Candidate A

(a) (ii) Energy = $4.18 \times 40 \times 34 = 5684.8\,J\,mol^{-1}$ (5680 to 3 significant figs)

Candidate B

(a) (ii) $\frac{4.18 \times 40 \times 34}{1000} = 5.6848\,kJ$

e Candidate A has the correct numerical answer but incorrect units. They should be joules, not 'joules per mole', as the amount of substance being dealt with is not 1 mole. This loses her 1 of the 2 marks. Candidate B has the correct units, but has not written his answer to the three significant figures required by the data. He scores 1 mark.

Candidate A

(a) (iii) $\frac{5680}{0.05} = -114\,000\,J\,mol^{-1}$

Thus $\Delta H = -114\,000\,J\,mol^{-1}$

Candidate B

(a) (iii) −113.696 kJ mol^{-1}

Candidate A has the correct answer with a suitable number of significant figures and the right sign. She scores 2 marks. Candidate B also scores 2 marks because he would not be penalised twice for a significant figure error. However, he would have been well advised to show his working. Note that the units include 'per mole' now.

Candidate A

(a) (iv) Plastic cup

Candidate B

(a) (iv) Glass beaker, surrounded by cotton wool, to avoid heat losses

Candidate A scores 1 mark only for 'plastic cup', though she has not given the reason (small specific heat capacity). Candidate B has given an alternative apparatus and justified his answer. He scores 2 marks.

Candidate A

(b) (i) Barium, because it's at the bottom.

Candidate B

(b) (i) Barium, because it has most electron shells.

Both candidates score 1 mark for barium. Candidate A's reason does not 'justify her answer' and she does not score the second mark. Candidate B scores the second mark for a good reason.

Candidate A

(b) (ii) Barium

Candidate B

(b) (ii) Barium, because it has the lowest ionisation energy.

Both candidates score the mark. No reason is asked for. So, while it is nice to see a reason from Candidate B, he would be best advised not to give one in case he gets it wrong, which might put his mark in jeopardy.

Candidate A

(b) (iii) Magnesium

Candidate B

(b) (iii) Magnesium carbonate

Both candidates score the mark, though Candidate A has answered the question more accurately.

Candidate A

(c) (i) Decomposition

Candidate B

(c) (i) Thermal decomposition

Candidate A does not score because she has not given the detail stressed in the specification. Candidate B has included the all-important word 'thermal' and scores the mark.

Candidate A

(c) (ii) The solid melts.

Candidate B

(c) (ii) The solid bubbles, gives off a brown gas and disappears.

Candidate A scores 1 mark for one of the possible answers. Candidate B starts with two other possible answers. However, he has added something that is inaccurate (barium oxide solid remains) so he is judged to be 'hedging his bets' and only 1 mark is awarded.

Candidate A

(c) (iii) Shake the gases with alkali, then only oxygen will be left.

Candidate B

(c) (iii) Collect the oxygen 'over water'. The nitrogen dioxide will dissolve.

Candidate A's method would be difficult to carry out, so it does not score. Candidate B is correct, for 1 mark.

Candidate A

(c) (iv) Molar mass of $Ba(NO_3)_2 = 261$
Moles of barium nitrate = 0.5
Therefore, volume = 12

Candidate B

(c) (iv) Moles of barium nitrate $= \frac{13}{261} = 0.05$

Volume of oxygen $= 0.05 \times 24 \times 0.5 = 0.6\,cm^3$

Candidate A does not score. She has calculated the molar mass of barium nitrate correctly but the mole calculation is wrong. She then heads for a mark on the 'error carried forward' principle, until she falls at the last hurdle by failing to give the units. Candidate B scores the first mark and is near the second until he writes down cm^3 rather than dm^3, presumably by mistake.

Overall, Candidate A scores 10 out of 19. Candidate B scores 16.